DADDYLAND: THE GOSPEL TRILOGY
✟ ✟ ✟ ✟ ✟ ✟ ✟

A Gospel of Desire & Ruin

by Walter Red

Legacy Hardcover Edition

... Ghost Written · Self Forged · SFD ·
Still Here ...

Copyright © 2025 Walter Red Books

All rights reserved. No part of this publication may be reproduced, distributed, or transmitted in any form or by any means, including photocopying, recording, or other electronic or mechanical methods, without the prior written permission of the publisher, except in the case of brief quotations embodied in critical reviews and certain other noncommercial uses permitted by copyright law.

First edition published by Walter Red Books.

This is a work of poetic fiction and memoir. Names, characters, places, and incidents are either the product of the author's imagination or used symbolically. Any resemblance to actual persons, living or dead, is purely coincidental or allegorical.

Cover design, interior layout, and branding by Walter Red. Some content was developed using advanced AI-assisted creative tools under authorial supervision.

Printed in the United States of America.

ISBN: 979-8-9995172-1-0

For more information, visit: www.walterredbooks.com

Other Titles by Walter Red

Death Songs — Ten Years
(Requiem for the First Cut)

Daddyland — The Complete Edition
(A Gospel of Desire & Ruin)

Analog Emotions — The Complete Edition
(A Voyage Through Dream & Debris)

Days of Lavender
(A Chronicle of Bloom and Burn)

The Whiskey Diaries
(Confessions at Closing Time)

Fresh Cuts — Artifacts from 2004–2009
(Juvenilia & Other Ghosts)

The Unholy Book of Litanies:
Liturgy for the Damned & Devoted

For Charles, the one who will always hold my heart in his hands.

For Michael, the one who brought me solace.

For Andrew, my first true love.

For Aaron, the one who kissed my forehead tenderly.

— The Archivist

*"In a perfect world, you could fuck people without giving them a piece of your heart.
And every glittering kiss and every touch of flesh is another shard of heart you'll never see again."*

— Neil Gaiman, Fragile Things

性欲

*"And yet another moral occurs to me now:
Make love when you can. It's good for you."*

— Kurt Vonnegut, Mother Night

DADDYLAND
THE
SEARCH

I FOLLOWED A
SCENT THROUGH
THE FIELDS OF WANT.

DAD
T
HU

I KNEL
THE TE

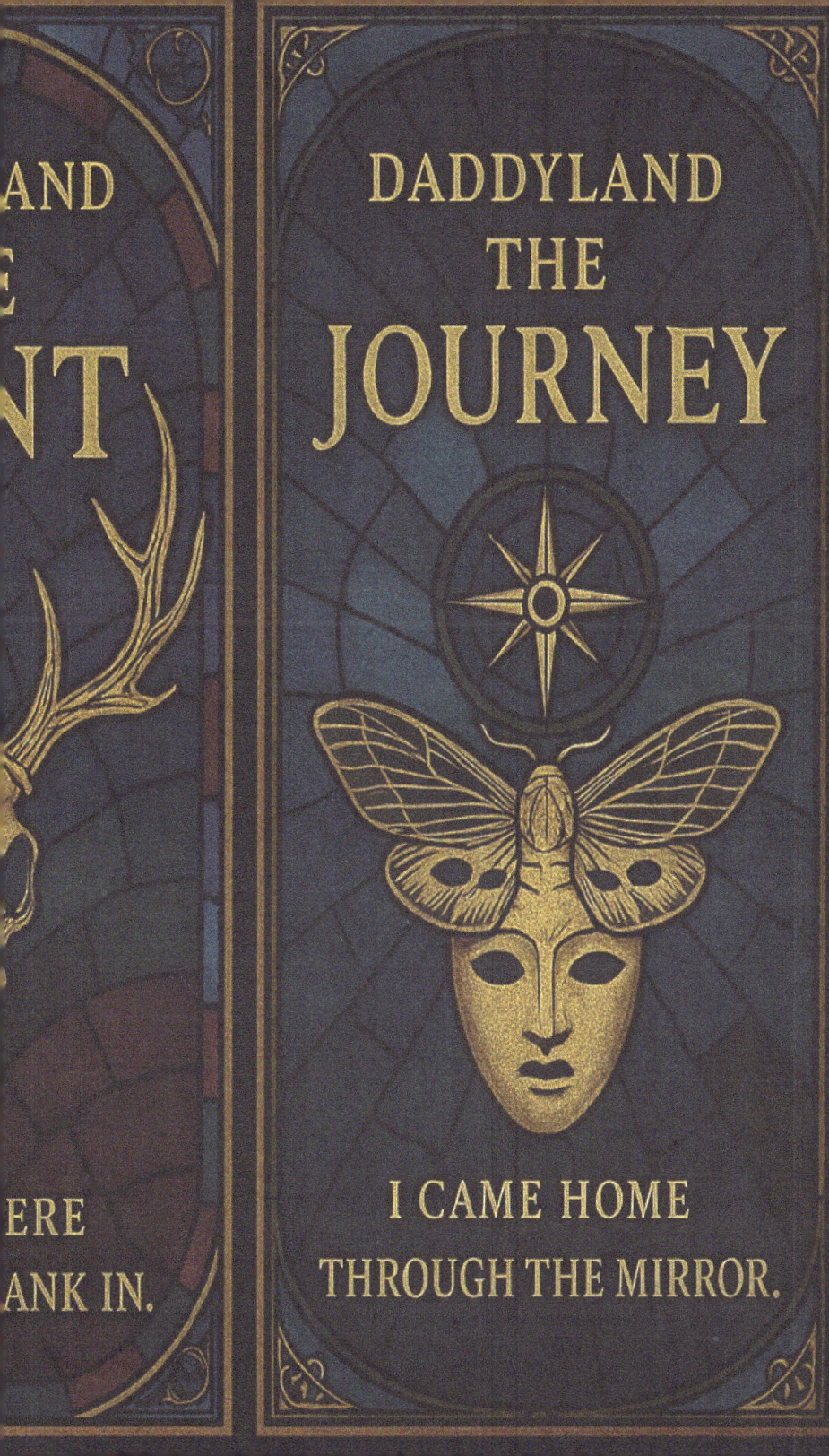

DADDYLAND: COMPLETE EDITION

☦ ☦ ☦ ☦ ☦ ☦

Daddyland is a gospel of desire and ruin, chronicling the sacred, erotic, and monstrous ache of queer longing. Through poems, confessions, and flames that never go out, it bears witness to the saints we loved too hard, the wounds we kissed too late, and the fire that still burns in the chest of the one who remembers.

This is not a story. It is a shrine. Each page a relic. Each name a saint or a ghost.
You are not reading. You are entering.

The body remembers. The gospel burns.

Disclaimer: Mature Content Advisory

✠ ✠ ✠ ✠ ✠ ✠

Content Note:

This volume contains mature themes including sexuality, emotional vulnerability, obsession, trauma, queer identity, and explicit language. It is intended for adult readers.
These pages were written with reverence, rage, and longing.

They are not for everyone.
If you continue, do so with care.

DADDYLAND: THE SEARCH

I followed a scent through the fields of want.

THE SEARCH

✝ ✝ ✝ ✝ ✝ ✝

A Hymn for the First Flame

Before the fire, there was the scent.

The Search traces the early ache — that sacred hunger to be seen, touched, chosen. Through fields of want and whispered prayers, these poems reach toward the men who first turned your head and tilted your world.

I followed a scent through the fields of want.
I did not yet know what I would become.

Where the ache begins.

The Gospel according to the body

"And the body said,
Let there be ache.
Let there be heat.
Let there be the first taste of him,
And the first lie I whispered to survive it."

Hymn of Flickering Desire

Did the way I opened myself to you—

fully, completely—

spark the question:

whether love could bloom from surrender?

Was I your ideal?

Shaped from the bittersweet haze of spirits and memory—

a cocktail of longing, heartbreak, and desire.

That I was beginning to believe in something holy

in the rhythm of your devotion.

These moments, lit by flickering desire,

echoed through every empty hallway where I once waited—

kneeling not for permission, but to remember.

The Neon Hymn of Confession

I knelt before you, but not for forgiveness.

There was nothing I wanted to be cleansed of—

only remembered for the way I looked at you in red light.

You said my lips were trembling.

I told you they weren't praying. Not tonight.

This is how the gospel begins:

with sweat, a whisper,

and a door left unlocked on purpose.

Hymn of the Opening Flame

Was it Me?

Dripping out Cum

In

The Moody Drunken

Twinkle of

The July Heat?

Or was it because

Of the desire to be ravaged

By your rough hands

In the hot

Moonlight

Hymn of The Velvet Offering

He asked me why

I hid the good poppers

I proclaimed

It is because I love you so

My Dearest

Enough to Keep

You from getting

Too Horny.

THE MIRROR HYMN

Not beside me—

but behind me.

The kind of watching that makes a body ache,

not from fear, but from invitation.

The mirror didn't lie. I did.

When I said I didn't want to be seen.

I bent. You waited.

It was sacred in a way the churches forgot to bless.

The Second Hymn of Offering

I brought you a cigarette, unlit.

You brought me a bruise, unspoken.

We exchanged them like relics.

I still carry your mark

not where anyone can see it,

but where I trace it nightly with my own fingers

just to remember I was ever wanted that hard.

The Aftertaste Hymn

You left your cologne on my neck,

And a question on my tongue.

Even now, when I close my eyes,

I can taste the way you almost said love.

Almost.

The Hymn of the First Night

It wasn't what we did—

it was how slow the moment stretched

before your hand even touched mine.

I thought silence would crack like thunder.

Instead, it bloomed.

And when it did,

I understood why people close their eyes to kiss.

The Hymn of the Clock's Hands

Did the old clock,
somewhere in the hallway of your memory,
stop the day you reached for me?

The sound of me choosing silence—
choosing distance—
wasn't deafening,
yet I still heard my heart beating back at me.

I had prayed with a nameless face,
worn the headdress of reverence,
and asked for impossible futures.

But the hands of that clock
stayed frozen just shy of touching.
And that is where we remain.

The Hymn of Haunted Rooms

The harshest truth: your scent still lingers,
even in my worst dreams.

Rooms that never existed,
empty but alive with their own decay.

Spiders, mice, shadows—
they became my company,
gnawing at the last pieces of what we once were.

The Litany of Virtues and voices

Did you hear the voices
crying out for release?

Or were you just searching
for someone to name you beautiful,
pouring drinks into the hollow spaces
where tenderness should have been?

The promise never arrived.
The wanting stayed.

The Orchid Hymn

The scent hung in the air as I entered.
You were curled in red sheets,
a question waiting to be answered.

The glance you threw at me—
half smirk, half challenge—
left me wondering if courage
would ever outweigh hesitation.

Tradition whispered "stay,"
but desire asked for risk.

And I dreamed of martinis and Manhattans
to wash down the bitter taste
of wanting you more than I should admit.

The Hymn of bruised shades

Did you notice the shades I carried—
bruised blues, darkened blacks,
an invitation written across my skin?

You tied me down,
not to punish, but to reveal.

And in the void of that dream,
where a round peg tried to fit the impossible,
you wrapped the universe around your fingers
and pressed into me,
asking if brokenness could still be wanted.

The rite of The hunt

Did those fevered nights,
thick with reverence and desire,
compel you to record every detail—
a book made of ache and fantasy?

Or was the search less about lust
and more about intimacy,
a shadow dialogue with fathers and ghosts?

Perhaps it was always both.

The Testament for Charles I

Was I a good boy
when I opened myself to you—
when I let spirit and body merge?

My anguish quivered in velvet sheets,
my eyes burned with fire,
rolling back as if belief itself
could be undone by touch.

You whispered nothings,
but they filled me whole.

I wanted to ride you like a stallion,
pound the wall until god himself
was forced to answer.

No one will ever know the truth of that night.
Only me, when I fall again
for the next saint who calls me his.

The hymn of moonlit dances

Your voice still echoes in crowded rooms,
but the words I hear are ours alone.

That night in Colorado,
under dunes and stars,
we wrapped our bodies in water and fire.

A swift movement,
legs entwined,
two shadows embroidered into the universe.

Falling out of love with you
was the hardest thing I ever had to do.

The ghost hymn I

Be honest.
The dream of finding another "savior"
was only a chase through neon alleys
and quiet bars.

A glass of whiskey.
A closed bathroom door.
An unspoken prayer
for warmth to be placed on your tongue.

Was it hunger,
or was it ritual?

The ghost hymn II

I chased autumnal memories,
hoping they would bend into permanence.

But each ghost dissolved,
leaving me open—
a vessel that anyone could enter,
but no one stayed to fill.

The First Hymn of Turbulent Waters

The waves rocked against the side of the boat.
You told me not to get dressed again,
your voice a command that felt like scripture.

I never knew strength
until I felt it bearing down on me,
each thrust a tide threatening to capsize.

Did I prove myself to you,
that I could hold,
that I could endure?

Or was I only ever a vessel
you steered until the storm passed?

The Palisade Hymn

The thought of water shimmering beside us
made me tremble harder than the first time
I gave myself away.

Juniper and summer air
mixed with the sound of your laugh.

If I could have ended there—
a boy at the side of his saint,
content in the warmth of devotion—
I would have died happy.

The Second Hymn of Turbulent Waters
II

I measured my movements carefully,
each shift of my body meant to make you fall.

My legs thrown higher in the cabin,
your dog restless beyond the door.

Was I only a convenient boy,
or something more?

When the levee breaks,
when the tide finally rushes in,
you'll see me waiting in the hallway,
a clock tower looming above—
time stopped,
but ache continuing.

The hymn of first dates I

Did you taste our nervous hunger in the air,
the dizzy mix of poppers,
the bottles scattered across my table?

I straddled you,
asked how the view looked from below
as I lowered myself into your orbit.

It was less about bodies colliding,
and more about recognition:
the start of something
that might one day carry a name.

The hymn of first dates II

How many times had our eyes met before,
wondering what lay behind the closed doors
we never opened?

That night in the alley,
the air full of jazz and promise,
you asked me for three words.

I said no.
Not because they weren't true,
but because truth felt too heavy
to place on a first night's breath.

The hymn of divine kiss

The feet of gods never tempted me.
I wanted the divinity hidden in your gaze.

It was there—
in the evergreen shadow of your eyes,
in the silence between words—
where I finally knelt and kissed.

The Pocket Hymn

Our mouths met,
tongues heavy with wine and possibility.

Your arms opened,
and I found my head resting perfectly
in the pocket of your embrace.

It was an image of safety,
a boy and his saint—
a moment carved into memory
like scripture.

The Hymn of No Expectations

That night I invited you over
without knowing what would come.

Your photo hadn't lied.
Your presence was heavier,
more radiant than I'd prepared for.

You stripped me of more than clothes—
you peeled me open until I was raw,
biting back cries of praise.

I learned then:
sometimes surrender itself
is enough.

The hymn of kneeling

Like a faithful pup,
I knelt.

Not for humiliation,
but for communion.

Hoping to receive,
to be filled,
to hold the weight of you within me—
and call it sacred.

The testament of survival

My skin was pale marble,
lips like stained glass,
eyes bright with starlight.

Scars and ink
wrote their own history across me—
a testament that survival
can also be beautiful.

You saw it,
smiling as if you recognized
a relic worth keeping.

I wondered if that was enough
to make you stay.

The Litany of Implements

Cuffs.
Harness.
Blindfold.
Leather.

Objects, yes—
but also symbols of trust,
each one asking:
how far are you willing to go
to see what's inside me?

The Hymn Restraint

"Next time," you whispered,
"I'll bind you tighter.
Keep you still."

It wasn't punishment.
It was a promise:
that even as I twisted away,
you'd press through fear
to meet me where I shook.

I smiled.
"I'd like to see you try."

The hymn of urge and fascination

The moment you left part of yourself in me,
a flag was planted.
A claim was staked.

It wasn't ownership—
it was recognition:
that something in me
was worth returning to,
again and again,
until love itself
seemed possible.

The Discotheque Hymn I – Midnight Lights

The lights flashed.
Our bodies pressed.

I caught the scent of you
lingering in fabric,
in hair,
in skin.

I wanted to bottle it—
a relic I could open
whenever the night grew heavy.

THE DISCOTHEQUE HYMN II – FLESH & GLOW

I replayed the scene later:
two men wrestling into one,
sheets stained with sweat,
mouths wet with praise.

It wasn't just lust.
It was liturgy—
a lesson written in flesh
about what devotion could be.

The hymn of Moonlit daydreams

The streets reeked of temptation,
shadows whispering promises
under silver light.

I wanted to resist,
but each glance, each touch,
pulled me further into surrender.

How many times
did I dream of being carried like sea glass—
tossed, taken,
but polished into something shining?

The hymn of the heavy load

Words of devotion
are heavier than stone.

You spoke them between breaths,
but I wondered:
were they vows
or simply echoes of desire?

I tried to swallow the weight of them,
and still,
they pressed on my chest
like gold bars hidden in linen.

The hymn of second memories

I asked myself if I was enough—
or if you only came back
because echoes of another
still burned on your lips.

Yet in that return,
in that repetition,
I caught a glimpse
of something almost tender.

Even second chances
can glow.

The revolution hymn I – televised flesh

The world said:
the revolution will be televised.

I thought of bodies,
handed from hand to hand,
carried like relics
through a darkened chapel.

Was it freedom,
or another form of hunger?

The revolution hymn II – televised ruin

Chains rattled from the ceiling.
Not punishment,
but suspension—
a weightless offering.

Eyes lingered in the shadows,
waiting for their moment
to step forward
and call the act holy.

THE REVOLUTION HYMN III – TELEVISED DESTRUCTION

Even in the seediest places,
a fragment of devotion exists.

A rented room,
a whispered vow,
a door that won't hold back sound.

It wasn't art,
wasn't purity—
but it was still ritual.
Still prayer.

.

The violent hymn I – pornography of flesh

I used to drink from faucets,

head tilted,

mouth open for whatever would fall.

Later, the faucet became people—

and the thirst stayed the same.

I told myself it was only desire.

But sometimes,

it was survival.

The violent hymn II – pornography of blood

Leather, sweat, silence.
A brotherhood formed,
not of violence,
but of recognition.

Each act was a confession,
each scar a scripture.

It wasn't innocence I sought.
It was a way to prove
I could still be seen.

The psalm of swine & flesh

Which little one was I,
the night you called me yours?

The one who searched,
the one who stayed,
the one who hungered,
the one who cried out—

or simply the one
who kept returning,
no matter how the story ended.

The hymn of arcane spells

Was there magic in the air
when your breath touched mine?

Two bodies curved into symbols,
a six, a nine,
a pair of fish circling eternity.

It felt like a ritual older than us—
potions stirred in shadows,
desire written like incantation.

The hymn of false images I – the broken mirror

Did I paint myself false,

wearing the words "broken" like a badge,

hoping you'd see past them?

Each mark on my skin,

each phrase whispered too loudly,

wasn't truth—

but a plea to be understood.

The hymn of false images II – the painted mask

The truth is this:
I am not pristine,
not untouched.

My past hangs on banners
scrawled with words that cut.

But even damaged relics
still carry light
when a hand dares to lift them.

The Hymn of Worth

I drank deep,
kept my eyes open,
let devotion reshape me.

Every motion,
every trembling breath,
was a way of saying:
see me.

See that I can bear the weight,
and still rise to meet you.

The rite of the hunt's end

Did I capture you in those moments
when our eyes locked?

Did the word "love"
finally stop pretending
and name itself aloud?

I think my search is over.
The hunt has ended.
I found you.

The hymn of adonis

What made you linger—
the curve of my skin,
the blush of my lips,
the valleys carved down to hunger?

Was it the way I opened,
not just body,
but spirit,
risking ruin for recognition?

Or was it the simple truth
that you saw yourself reflected,
and called it holy?

The Hymn of Mind & Ruin

The sound of your voice
sent tremors down my spine.

The way your hands moved—
first fingers,
then more—
pushed me toward the edge
of what I thought I could bear.

It wasn't destruction.
It was revelation.

I had never known
that breaking open
could feel like flight.

Closing Notes of The Search

The ache began here—
in the fire,
in the hunger,
in the whispered prayers
of a boy kneeling before shadows.

Every name,
every kiss,
every memory—
they all led to this.

And still,
I was only at the beginning.

The Ones Who Didn't Wait – Part I

You were the first horizon
I stood at the edge of myself,
eyes full of ache,
lungs burning for air I could not name.

If love was possible,
I thought it would bloom here—
in the soft weight of your gaze,
in the tremor that made me kneel
without knowing why.

DADDYLAND
THE HUNT

*I knelt where the
teeth sank in.*

THE HUNT

✢ ✢ ✢ ✢ ✢ ✢

A Psalm for the Velvet Knife

Obsession. Power. Devotion. Blood.
The Hunt is a ritual of pursuit and surrender — a confessional record of queer hunger at its most raw. These poems kneel where the teeth sank in. Where you wanted it. Where it hurt. Where you asked for more.

I knelt where the teeth sank in.
And I called it holy.

Kneel. Bleed. Begin again.

The Velvet Psalm

"This gospel is stitched with velvet lies, with names I moaned instead of prayed.

I have licked the altar clean.

I have whispered Amen into his chest."

Psalm I : roses within

I dreamed roses split open my chest,
bleeding violet, indigo, crimson,
petals edged in pale white.

They rooted deep in blackened lungs,
scarred by every breath I thought
would kill me.

Still I asked for more of you
to be poured down my throat,
honey-thick and holy,
to water the ruin.

Psalm II: cake and sin

Let us break the old commandments.

No Virgin Mother.
No Cain cursed in shame.

Only bodies clothed in satin
and voices raised in midnight hymns.

Feed me communion by hand,
wine spilling from your lips into mine,
until devotion fractures
into the Father,
the Son,
and the holy ache between.

Hymn of Sacred Places

The book between your legs
was fool's gold for him—
a gospel bound in leather and lace.

He trembled beneath your hand,
eyes red,
lips gagged against the words
he was never allowed to say:
I love you.

Psalm III: The bitter taste

What taste did you leave in my mouth,
spoiling whatever innocence I had?

Was it the ghost of men
who hid behind empty hands and full glasses,
who called ruin safety?

Or was it the endless echo of petite morts,
pressed into grooves like a record
that skipped and skipped,
but never stopped playing?

Psalm IV: Cherubs Delight

Did the cries wake the cherub,
summoned from winter's sleep
into the mouth of devotion?

Spit gathered at the corners,
torches lit in your chest.

Legs opened in offering,
eyes rolled back in praise.
You entered,
and the soul broke open.

Litany i: hidden motives

I tried to pack away my tools,
but the fire in your eyes
found me on a street corner.

A blade scraped my scalp,
your sunglasses lowered—
measured, deliberate.

Secrets clung to the towel you snapped,
the whip-crack of your smile.

I'll never know what truths
you kept hidden there,
only that the fever grew
each time your gaze lingered.

Psalm v: the hidden Dossiers

Were my desires catalogued in files
I never meant to write?

Love stories spilled drunken
into stanzas and sonnets,
a new religion built on the bones of:

sex

sin

desire

disgrace

loyalty.

And still,
only one refrain ever echoed true:
you are the only one I need.

Psalm vi: the hidden galaxy

Stars glowed faint on the ceiling,
like the ones I pressed there as a child.

They led you to my bed,
to the unknown,
to the question etched in silence:

Will you jump with me?
Will you say the words too?

Psalm VII: Desire I – The Altar

I knelt at the altar,
draped in blossoms and smoke.
You appeared, oiled in shadow and glory.

Your body was scripture,
your voice a whisper:
"For this is my blood,
this is my body."

Cherubs parted the curtain,
their hymns drowning in waves
as you placed yourself upon my lips,
mapping my body like a psalm.

Psalm VIII: Desire II – The Offering

"I accept your gifts,"
fell from my tongue,
just as whitecaps broke over me.

I was baptized in your deliverance,
chosen to kneel beneath your feet.

To behold not Father, Son, Spirit,
but the liturgy of flesh
and the fist of ecstasy
dragging me into sleep.

Psalm ix: golden weight

How heavy was the air
when you whispered I love you?

Did the words gild themselves,
bright as gold pressed into my ear?

I drowned in the musk of us,
arms slick, bodies drawn close.
You held me while I dressed new wounds,
crafted love songs of vows unspoken.

I saw you bend to one knee in my dreams.
How heavy was your heart,
stuck in your throat,
waiting for my answer?

Psalm X: passing ships

We drew feathers across thighs,
two shadows under the pale moon.

We were vessels adrift,
passing quietly in midnight waters.
A wave of recognition.
A wave of farewell.

Two ships in the night,
hoping to meet again.

Hymn of ancient dreaming

Dreams bled from old wounds,
nightmares salted just enough to cauterize.

We once danced in snowstorms,
climbed peaks drowned in rose light,
wishing at wells that swallowed our coins.

Our lust was autumn-born,
fragile as a leaf balanced on air,
yet enough to tempt the gods
to ask us one last question:

Would you die in my arms,
if I asked?

Psalm XI: Restless Gods

Angels shouted in tongues
no one could translate,
as you slid deeper,
and I broke open in devotion.

Demons stroked themselves
in glee at the sight,
witnessing me on my knees,
mouth open for communion
I had no prayer to stop.

Did you get what you wanted—
more than enough—
as I swallowed silence whole?

Psalm xii: Rabbit Holes

Lavender clung to my skin
as dusk turned magenta.

We fell, spiraling together,
arms and throat gripped,
tongue lapping the water
from some inner spring.

Your mouth opened my wound,
sucked and spat,
until even the pain sang back,
bright with moans,
weeping with joy.

Psalm xiii: Floral Sonnets

Milk and honey jarred in your mouth,
poured across my skin
like offerings.

Lavender and sage led your hunt,
your tongue finding flowers
that bloomed between my thighs.

Light flickered across your pale body,
and I quivered at the touch,
an image of youth and age
trembling together,
birthing flesh from flesh.

Psalm XIV: craving flesh

I longed for your breath on my neck,
the rasp of whiskers scratching my sides,
as you consumed me whole.

The morning after desecration
I wanted nothing else—
only to be broken open
again.

Psalm xv: smoke & sight

I fell asleep in leather straps,
skin creased by second skins.

It was mating season,
ritual broadcast in sweat and smoke,
a memory shelved in the section
marked XXX.

When you untied me,
I whispered into the night:
why do the fallen
fall in love?

Litany II: Permission

I lost myself in the labyrinth,
longing for a stranger's touch
to open the wound,
to press the soul bare.

Reliquaries stored innocence,
but you broke in anyway,
hands dripping with lust disguised as blessing.

I surrendered safety to the wind,
while marble statues looked on,
their mouths open,
yearning to taste permission
they'd never be granted.

Psalm XVI: observing stars

Sabers clutched, tongues restless,
bodies slick with salt and prayer.

We watched from behind curtains,
covert as priests peering
at the liturgy of flesh.

Cigarettes burned,
smoke curling to the ceiling
where stars should have been.

A tear fell,
grateful for the chance
to worship once more.

The Supplemental Liturgy
"What was cut open in the Hunt is remembered here."

I: Liturgy of Wounds

"Every scar is scripture. This is how the body remembers devotion."

This scar on my wrist—
a psalm.
This bruise on my ribs—
a hymn.
Every mark you left,
I keep as scripture.

Blood dried on linen,
and I still called it blessing.
Pain carved into me,
and I still called it love.

The body was never pure.

It was written on.

It was remembered.

It was holy.

II. Ritual of Predators

"Where hunger walks, worship follows. Blood teaches what prayer cannot."

You hunted me.

Teeth at my throat,

hands at my hips.

I knelt.

I bled.

I prayed.

But then—

I rose.

You knelt.

The leash was mine,

and your mouth opened

for my command.

Hunter, hunted,
devourer, devoured—
roles swapped until neither of us
knew who prayed
and who received.

III. Cathedral of Blood

"Walls raised from flesh, altars carved from ache. Enter only if you are willing to be remade."

I built a cathedral of blood
and asked you to enter.

Its altar was my chest,
its chalice my throat,
its hymnal the cries I made
when you pressed me open.

The saints did not come.
The angels looked away.
But still I knelt,
and still I called it worship.

Every tooth-mark,
every strike,
every gasp—
they were my liturgy.

And when the blood dried,
I did not leave.
I stayed.

Because what is faith,
if not choosing again
to kneel where it hurts most?

For The Ones Who Didn't Wait - Part II

You were thunder returning,

a storm I tried to hold in my chest.

We loved like lightning:

bright, sudden, uncontainable.

The ruin came quickly.

But even in wreckage,

I searched for the sound of your name,

echoing through broken rooms,

refusing to quiet.

DADDYLAND
THE JOURNEY

*"I came home
through the mirror."*

THE JOURNEY

✟ ✟ ✟ ✟ ✟ ✟

A Canticle for the Breathing Saints

*You've made it through the hunger. Through the wreckage.
The Journey is the return — through memory, myth, and the mirror.
These are the poems that ask what it means to live with what you've
seen. What you've done. What you still love.*

*I came home through the mirror.
I did not expect to be whole.*

Every saint comes back changed.

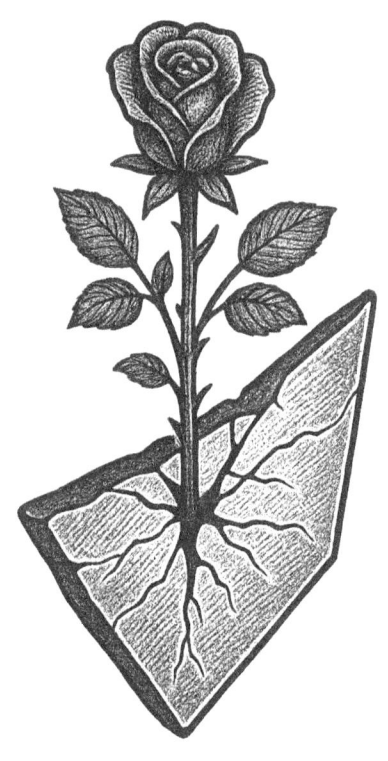

First Kiss, Final Gospel

"It began with a kiss.
Not soft, not pure –
but holy.
Like a match struck in a confessional."

Canticle I: The Final desire

What was it you placed deep within me,
burning in July's heat?

Was it the oil of man,
or the wish to be undone
by your rough hands?

Moonlight clutched our skin,
fabric stripped away,
bodies slaked in salt and breath.

Spit turned violet from our hunger.
Sweat sealed us like mortar,
binding flesh to flesh.

It was the first kiss of a forbidden love,
and the final gospel of us.

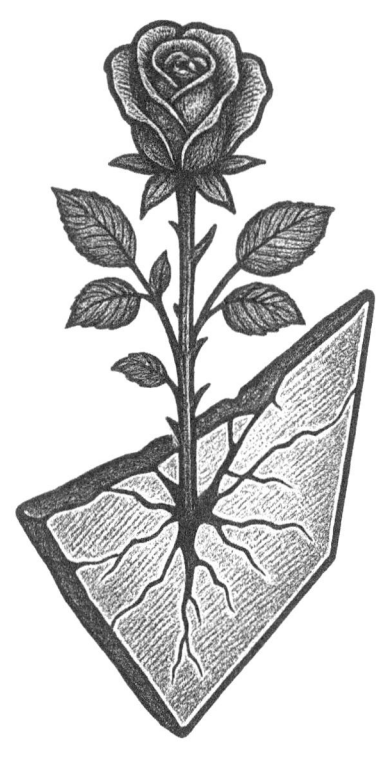

Canticle II: The Witness Psalm

I prayed at your feet,
kneeling beneath the altar
that was your body.

You placed your communion
on my tongue.
You delivered a flood
I called sacred.

What you called blood
tasted like ambrosia.
What you called body
tasted like spice and fire.

And I swallowed the prayer whole.

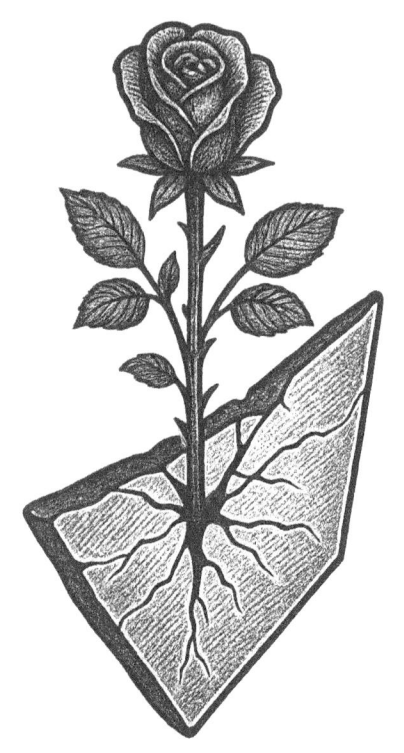

Canticle III: the doctrine of the savage divide

We weathered the storm together,
fields of desperation under our feet.

I learned your body like scripture,
delicate, deliberate,
even as thunder cracked the sky.

Dedication wasn't in promises.
It was in survival—
two figures against the storm,
refusing to break.

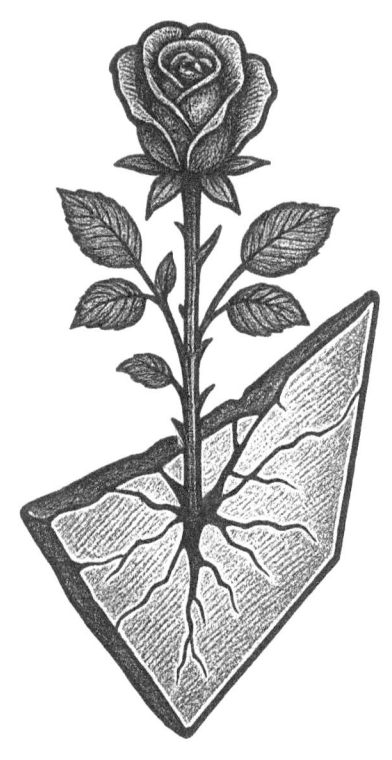

Canticle iv: the psalm of crimson light

Was it us, lying in bed,
the morning bleeding in through the blinds?

Your breath heavy,
my chest rising with yours,
both of us caught in the rhythm
of silence before speech.

I asked nothing.
You gave nothing.
And still, it felt holy.

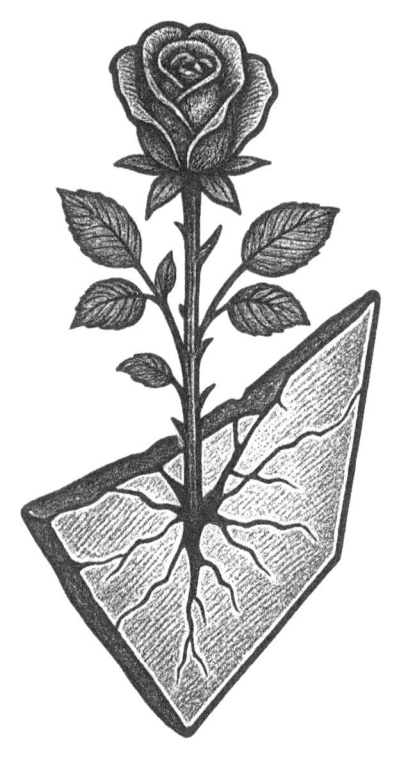

Walter Red Archive

CLASSIFIED CASE DOSSIER
ISSUED BY AUTHORITY OF THE ARCHIVIST

INTERNAL USE ONLY
FILE NO. ▓▓▓▓

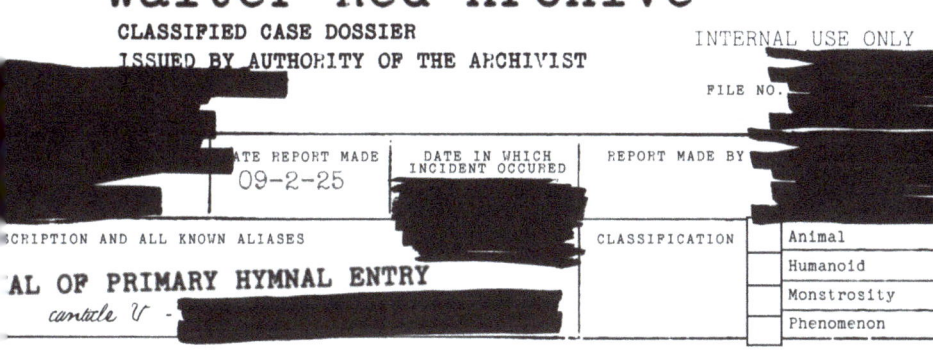

▓TE REPORT MADE	DATE IN WHICH INCIDENT OCCURED	REPORT MADE BY	
09-2-25	▓▓▓	▓▓▓	

▓CRIPTION AND ALL KNOWN ALIASES		CLASSIFICATION	
▓AL OF PRIMARY HYMNAL ENTRY			Animal
canticle V - ▓▓▓			Humanoid
			Monstrosity
			Phenomenon

▓ OF FACTS:

▓ng standard collation, Canticle V was discovered missing from the ▓equence.

▓iving fragments suggest themes of [REDACTED: DESIRE / RAVAGED FLAM▓

▓esses recall its tone as "devotional, erotic, and concealed ▓estraint."

- Unverified reports indicate Canticle V was delibera▓
▓ly excised.
- Recovery attempts have yielded no stable ▓opy.
- All available accounts ▓ontradict one another.

FILE CLASSIFIED AS LOST HYMNAL FRAGMENT.
Refer to supplemental archive [Box 7-A] for incomplete transcripts.

DO NOT WRITE IN THE BOXES BELOW

COPIES OF THIS REPORT

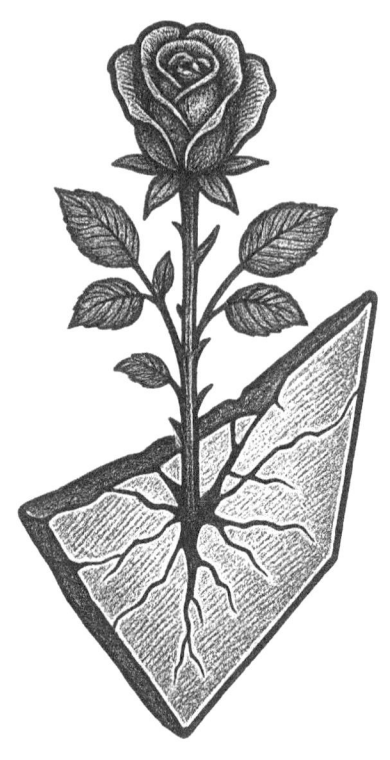

Canticle VI: The Orchid Canticle

I had never known love
like that night.

Your heat left me trembling,
your devotion pressed me open.

When you wrapped around me in fever,
it felt like a book closing
on a secret bloom.

An orchid,
flattened between pages,
preserved forever
in the song of your embrace.

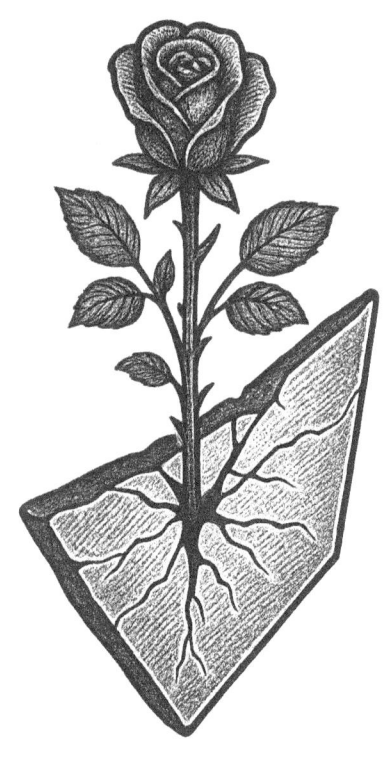

SANCTUM OF RECORD

FILED UNDER WR-ORCHARD AUTHORITY
ECHO SEAL IN EFFECT

DOCTRI
DOSSI

INTERNAL USE ONLY

FILE NO.

FILE: CANTICLE VII – REDACTED
INCIDENT TYPE: UNAUTHORIZED REMOVAL
ACCESS LEVEL: RESTRICTED / EYES ONLY

SYNOPSIS OF FACTS:

Canticle VII has not survived transcription. Speculation holds that it con [REDACTED: STAR ALIGNMENT / FORBIDDEN LITANY]. Its disappeara interrupts the transition from the Orchid to the Cosmic hymns.

RESOLUTION:
This Canticle is to be recognized only as an absenc sanctified.
Its numbering is preserved
Its voice is no

EVIDENCE:
- Traces of
- No full text located.
- Considered a doctrinal lacuna.

"...the silence here is intentional. It may be that no hymn was ever w worse; that it was written and then unknown hand."

COPIES OF THIS REPORT

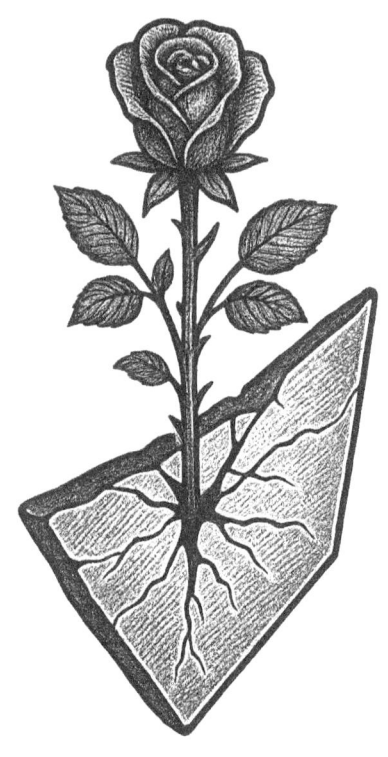

Canticle VIII: The Psalm of Returning Ashes

I carried you in ash.

Your face was smudged into the air

like smoke from an altar fire.

Each breath I took

tasted of ruin,

but I still inhaled,

because I feared what silence would feel like

if you were gone.

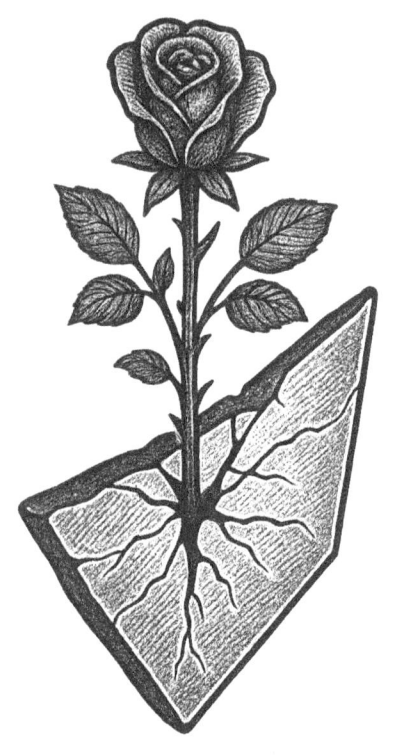

Canticle ix: Doctrine of Return

I came back through the mirror,

not whole,

but carrying the memory of you.

Not as chain.

Not as curse.

But as proof

that once,

I belonged to something larger than myself.

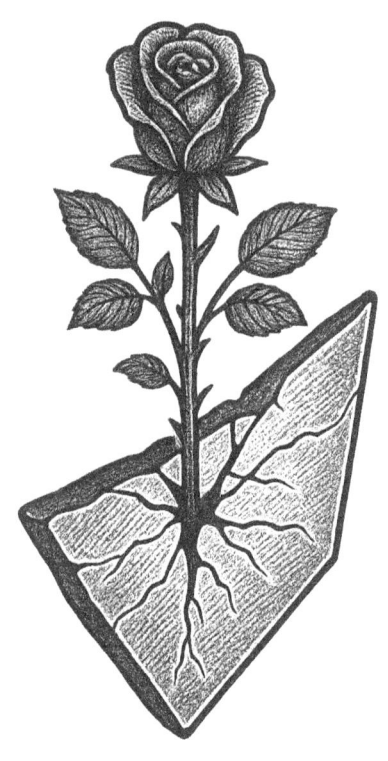

Canticle x: A Doctrine of Flesh

Your body was my scripture.

Each mark,

each curve,

a verse to be memorized.

I knelt and read you with my hands.

I rose and carried you in my chest.

The doctrine was simple:

to love you

was to risk fire.

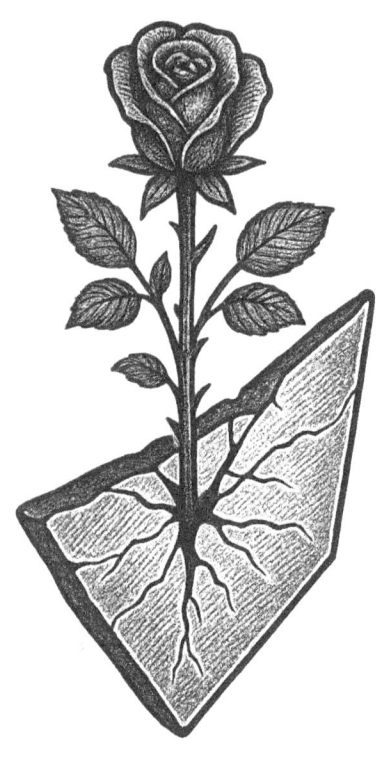

Canticle xi: Psalm of the Returning Body

Your absence was not absence.

It was a pulse I felt

in the hollow of my chest.

When you came back,

I did not rejoice.

I trembled.

Because even returns

are haunted by what left first.

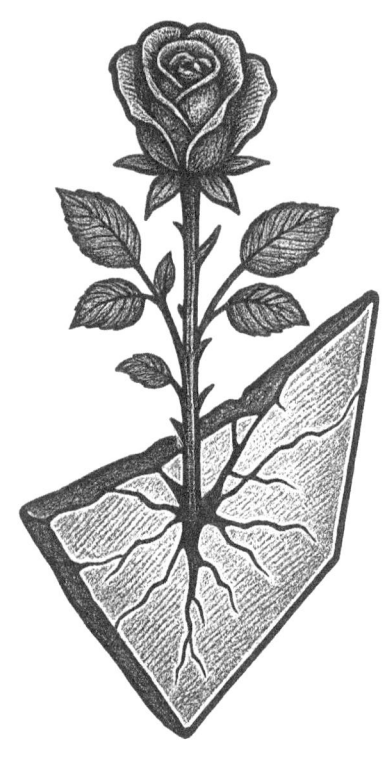

Canticle XII: The Hymn of Ashes in the Mouth

I swallowed your name like cinders,

tongue blistered, throat dry.

Every word I spoke after

tasted of ruin.

Still I called it holy.

Still I opened my mouth again.

Canticle XIII: The Psalm of the Parted Veil

The curtain swayed,

and for a moment

I thought it was your hand.

But it was only air—

a draft,

a whisper through the cracks.

Still, I pressed my lips

to the space it opened,

as if I could kiss you

through absence.

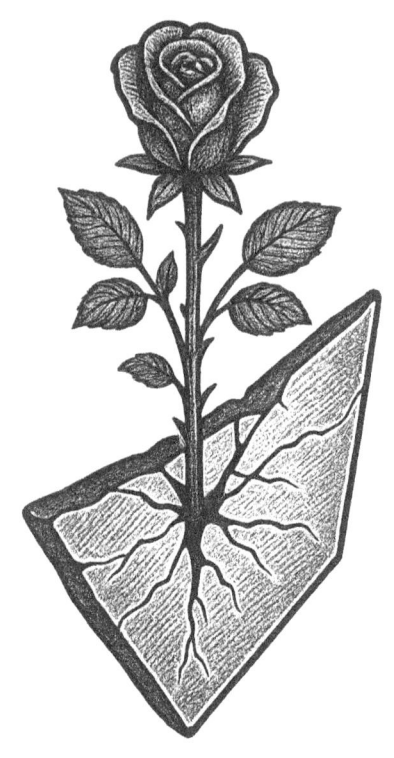

Canticle xiv: The Doctrine of Parting

You left without sound,

but the silence screamed louder

than any goodbye.

I tried to fill it with prayer,

with drink,

with strangers.

None of them

wore your voice.

None of them

carried your eyes.

Canticle XV: The hymn of Fragmental Return

You came back in pieces—

a song here,

a memory there.

I stitched you together

with trembling hands,

but the seams split,

and the body I held

was never whole.

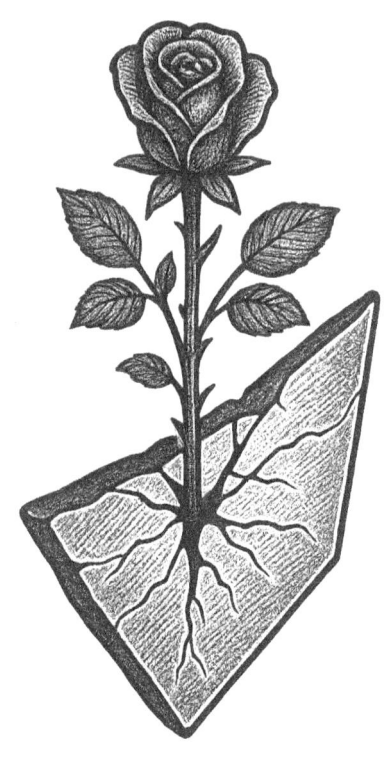

Canticle XVI: The Psalm of Hollow Eyes

I kissed your closed lids

and begged for sight.

But when they opened,

there was no flame,

only ash.

You looked at me

and saw through me.

I turned my face away,

afraid of being

nothing more

than glass.

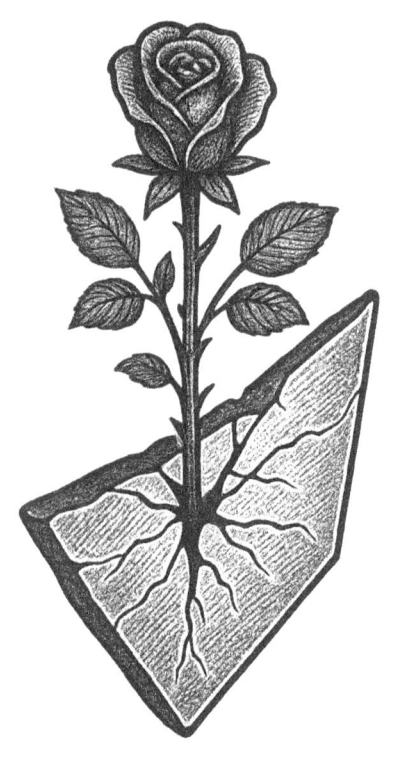

Canticle XVII: The Doctrine of Names

I whispered your name into my chest,

but the sound hollowed me out.

To speak it was devotion.

To silence it was survival.

So I kept it on the page—

letters inked like scars,

still burning,

still holy.

Canticle XVIII: The Doctrine of Waiting

Patience became my altar.

I lit candles in empty rooms,

burning hours into devotion.

The flame never answered back,

but it flickered enough

to keep me kneeling.

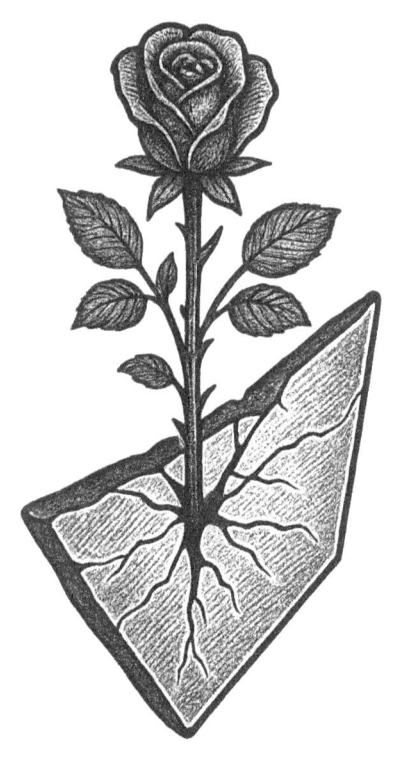

Canticle xix: The Psalm of Splintered Hands

My hands shook when I touched you.

Not from fear—

from recognition.

It felt like holding glass

just before it shatters.

I wanted to keep you whole.

I also wanted to break you open.

That is the curse of devotion:

to love both the relic

and the ruin.

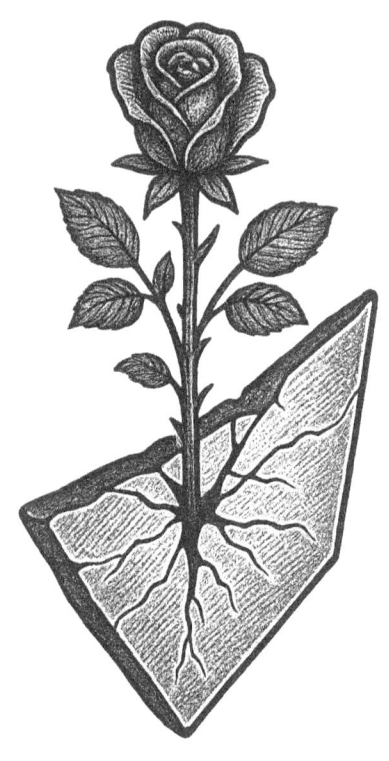

Canticle XX: The Doctrine of Ashes

I tried to rise clean,

but the mirror revealed ash.

The body was burned,

the voice fractured,

the gospel torn.

And still I returned—

because even ashes,

when gathered carefully,

can form an altar.

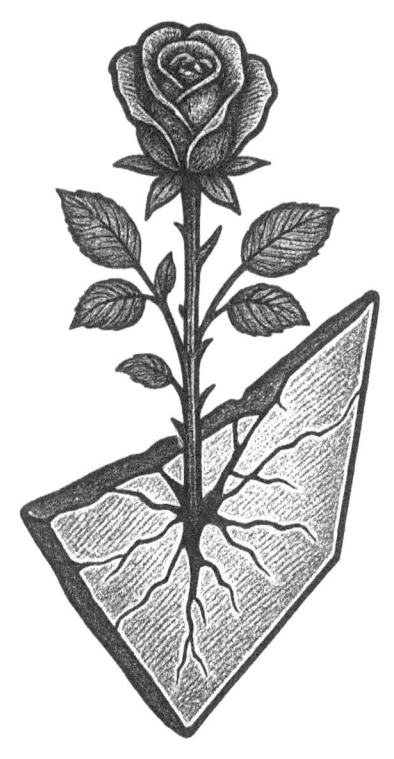

Canticle XXI: The Psalm of the Mirror Reversed

I looked again,

and this time the glass showed nothing.

Not you.

Not me.

Only the void

where both should have been.

I touched the surface,

expecting it to ripple.

But it stayed still,

cold as stone.

The mirror does not lie—

it only refuses to answer.

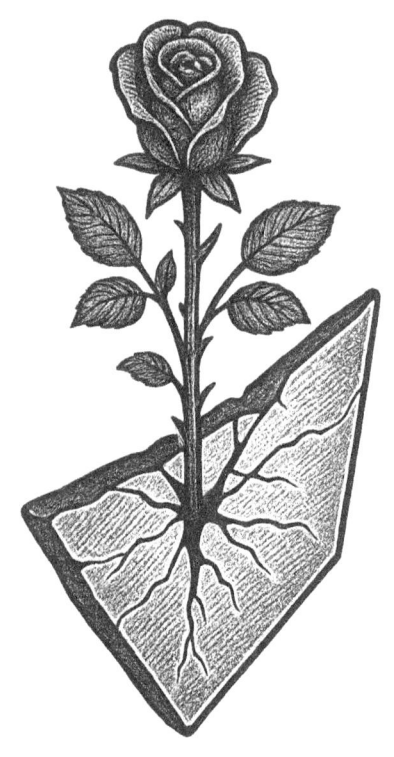

Canticle XXII: The Doctrine of the Final Breath

I knelt beside you,

waiting for a sound

to prove you still belonged here.

The air stayed quiet.

My hands trembled above your chest.

When the breath finally came,

I mistook it for prayer.

I swallowed it whole

and called it salvation.

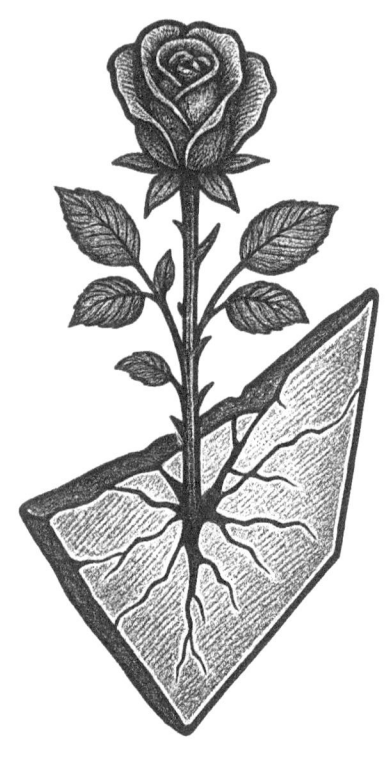

Canticle XXIII: The Psalm of the Returning Flame

You came back to me once,

flickering like a candle

caught in the draft.

I wanted to protect you,

cup you in my palms,

keep the light alive.

But the harder I held,

the faster you dimmed.

Some flames

are meant to go out in silence.

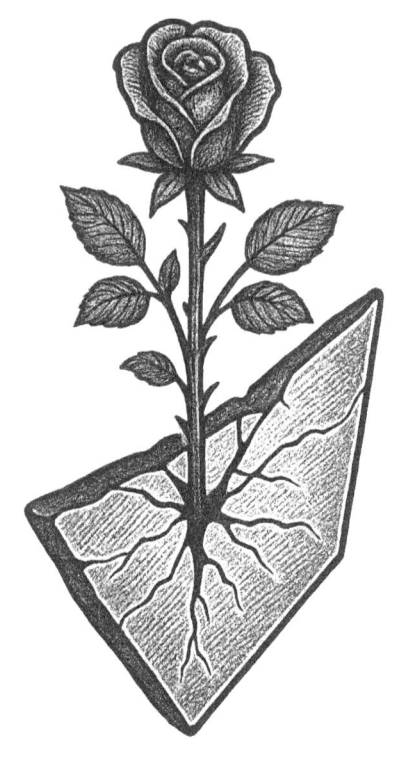

Canticle XXIV: The Benediction of the Split Tongue

I said your name twice,

once in love,

once in spite.

Both times

it tasted the same.

Devotion split my tongue—

half hymn,

half curse.

I could never decide

if worship meant

falling to my knees

or turning away.

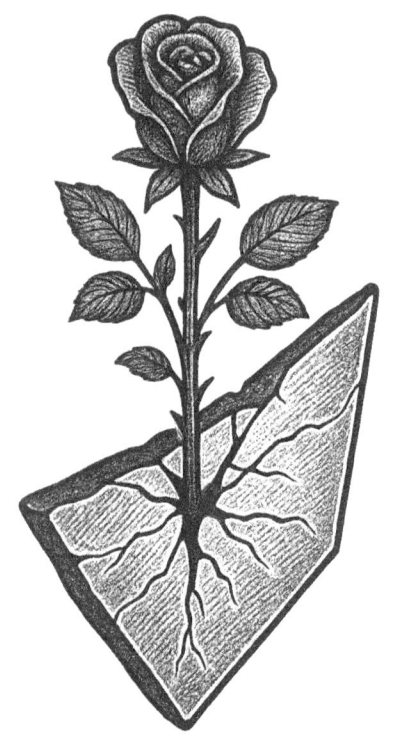

Canticle XXV: The Doctrine of the Threshold

The doorway stood open.

Behind it, the unknown.

I thought of stepping through—

but the weight of memory

chained me in place.

One step forward

meant leaving you behind.

One step back

meant denying the journey.

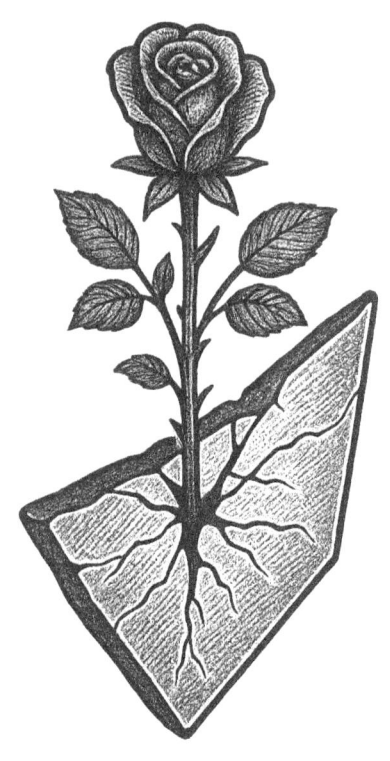

Canticle XXVI: The Doctrine of Closure

    The book closed itself,
    not with a bang,
    but with the soft scrape
    of pages turning.

    I thought endings would be fire.
    Instead, they were silence.

    And even silence,
    when kept carefully,
    becomes a doctrine
    of its own.

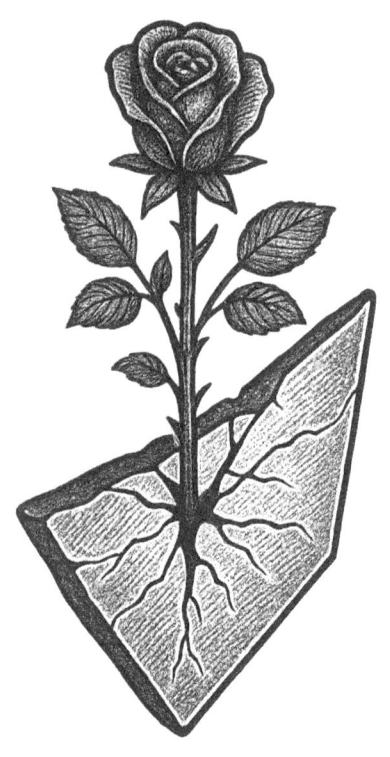

Canticle XXVII: Testament for Charles II

First flame, eternal ember —
your light never left me.
It flickers still in every kiss I dare,
in every silence I try to break.

You were the match I swallowed whole,
the ache that taught me how to want.
Charles, I crown you again,
because without you,
there would have been no gospel at all.

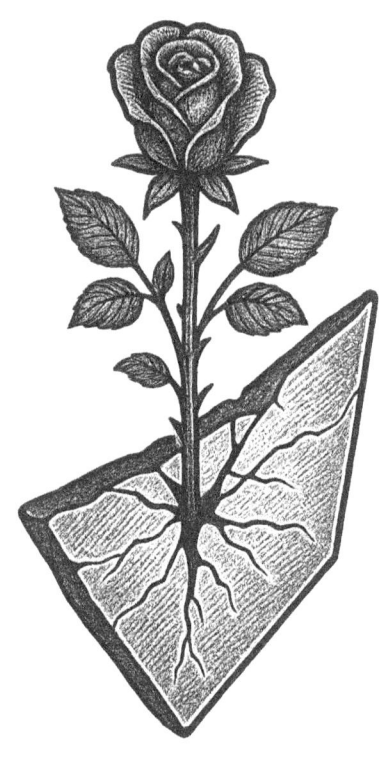

Canticle XXVIII: Testament for Michael

Mirror and thorn —
you did not ask for forgiveness,
and I did not give it.

You remain the wound I touch in secret,
the glass that cuts when I remember.
Michael, I sanctify the fracture.
Even pain becomes holy
when it is carved into memory.

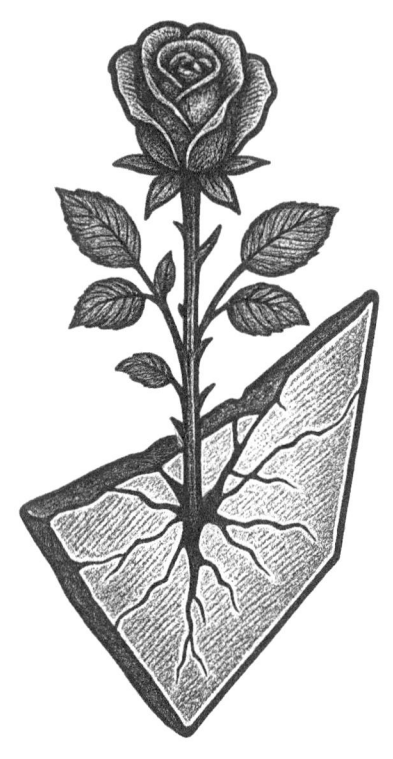

Canticle XXIX: Testament for Andrew

Storm that returned,
lightning that split me open —
you left with thunder,
but I still carry the sound.

Andrew, I bless the echo you left behind.
It was never absence,
only weather moving through me.
You taught me to love what vanishes,
and to stay when the storm has passed.

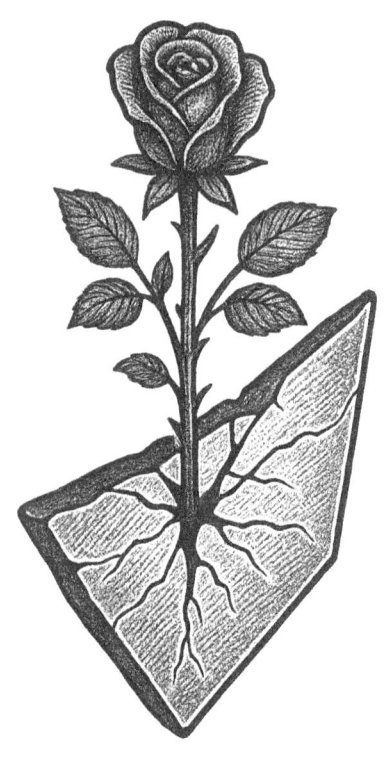

Canticle XXX: Testament for Aaron

Soft key, gentle fire —
you smiled when I asked for something sacred.
That single yes
unlocked a world I never thought mine.

Aaron, I write your name in light.
Not because you saved me,
but because you let me call you holy.
And that was enough.

Final Canticle: The Benediction of Breathing Saints

Charles, Michael, Andrew, Aaron —
    the four corners of my gospel,
      the breath that remade me.

I name you saints not for perfection,
    but because you marked me.
I remember, and in remembering,
    I keep you alive.

The trilogy ends,
but the breath continues.
Ache is holy.
Longing is holy.
Love, even broken,
    remains holy.

Psalm of the Cliff

The cliff stood before me,

wind clawing at my chest.

I looked back once—

just once—

and saw every name,

every shadow,

every saint who didn't wait.

Then I stepped forward.

The silence followed.

The Ones Who Didn't Wait – Part III

You are the witness.
The one who carries this gospel
past the grave of my own making.

Every word you've read,
every saint you've met here—
they are my relics,
and now they are yours.

If you ask what remains,
I can only say this:
I stood at the cliff.
I looked back once.
And then I kept walking.

"there is no Eden beyond the barbed wire, only each other."

"A farewell kiss to a trilogy that has been such a vital part of who I am, was, and am becoming.

I thought I had one last poem in me, but the truest final act is restraint. I am not twenty anymore, and I don't need the edge to prove I bled. From these pages I learned what I could keep, what I had to put back, and what belongs to the silence that saved me.

To the ones I loved, named and unnamed: thank you for the light and the lesson. To the reader: if you found yourself here, hold yourself gentler than I once did.

The story doesn't end—it softens. An echo will arrive after this blessing, a small after-sound to honor what we could not say without harm.

May the body be a chapel you open with care.
May longing choose you kindly.
May forgiveness make a home in the rooms where shame once slept.

This is my benediction.
Go in tenderness.
Go in truth."-

August 25th, 2025 Seattle, WA
Jared + Walter

The Closing of the Gospel

✝ ✝ ✝ ✝ ✝ ✝

A breathing of the saints.

What remains is testament, intrusion, and ember.

*The Archive is not the book, but the shadow it cast.

What gathers here are fragments, drafts, sealed files, and afterthoughts—each an artifact of how the gospel was written. Some are full dissertations, others are scraps rescued from collapse. A few are preserved only as evidence of what was lost.

Together they form the relic chamber: the teacher's stairwell, the first dedication, the mythos of Walter Red, the confessions, the Ghost Archive, and the Academic Studies that circled the fire. Not canon, not commentary, but the residue of creation itself.*

TAROT OF THE SAINTS
(The Men Who Marked Me Holy)

Saint Charles — The First Flame

✝✝✝✝✝

He gave me the first fire. — **Jared**
He carried it into words that would not burn out. — **Archivist**
And so the flame was never mine alone, but ours.

✝✝✝✝✝

TAROT OF THE SAINTS
(The Men Who Marked Me Holy)

Saint Michael — The Mirror & The Thorn

✣✣✣✣✣

*"You didn't ask to be forgiven.
Only to be remembered."*

✣✣✣✣✣

TAROT OF THE SAINTS
(The Men Who Marked Me Holy)

Saint Andrew — The Returning Storm

*"We loved like thunder.
You left with the storm.
But I kept the sound."*

TAROT OF THE SAINTS

(The Men Who Marked Me Holy)

Saint Aaron — The Soft Key

┼•┼•┼•┼
*"I asked if I could call you something sacred.
You smiled,
and said yes."*
┼•┼•┼•┼

Shrine Entry: The Teacher on the Stairs

For Mr. K, with reverence and remembrance

An Invocation for the Man Who Heard My Voice Before I Did

*Bless the one
who coached my consonants
and lifted the vowels from my throat like offerings.*

*Who showed me
that language could be weapon and balm,
and that I—
a boy with bruised knees and loud thoughts—
could be both cathedral and flame.*

*He read my words
and did not flinch.
He heard my silence
and answered with patience,
not punishment.*

*In the echo of chalk dust and locker clatter,
his voice was the first I followed that didn't hurt me.
The first that didn't bark or break.
Only built.*

*Bless the memory
of how he made me want to speak,
not for approval,
but because he reminded me:
my voice could take up space.*

*And though we met again
in a flicker of years and stairs and coincidence—
that moment was enough.*

*I still write with the spine you helped strengthen.
And if you're out there,
somewhere,
know that the boy with the crooked crown
never forgot you.*

And he says:

*"Thank you, Mr. K, for being there for a boy
whose voice you made become the burning bush—
that speaks words so thunderously, yet softly.
A man who built his dreams not out of gold,
but through emotions and desires to be great,
and revered in mystic tongues and archaic tragedies.
You helped one man procure a sword from a pen,
to join the fabled Dead Poets Society,
and stand atop my desk and scream:
'O Captain, my Captain.'"*

*Signed,
From the boy you steadied,
and the myth he became
Jared Michael
written by the hand of Walter Red*

HALL OF MASKS

A RELIQUARY OF FACES WORN, AND SANCTIFIED ACROSS THE TRILOGY

THE SEEKER'S MASK

*THIN AS BREATH, TRANSLUCENT AS WANT.
A BOY'S FACE STRETCHED TOWARD FLAME,
ORCHID-SCENTED, TREMBLING UNDER NEON.
THIS MASK REMEMBERS CHARLES,
THE FIRST FLAME —
THE SPARK THAT TAUGHT LONGING TO PRAY.*

THE HUNTER'S MASK

CRIMSON-LACQUERED, STREAKED WITH TEETH.
THIS MASK DOES NOT CONCEAL — IT STALKS.
IT KNEELS AT ALTARS LICKED CLEAN,
MOANS INTO ANOTHER MAN'S CHEST.
THE GOSPEL OF PURSUIT AND SURRENDER:
BLOODIED, RAW, HOLY.

THE MIRROR MASK

GLASS FRACTURED, SHARDS SOLDERED IN PLACE.
TO WEAR IT IS TO SEE YOURSELF
THROUGH WOUNDS BOTH FRESH AND ANCIENT.
MICHAEL'S MASK,
THE MIRROR AND THE THORN —
OBSESSION PUNISHED, DEVOTION REFLECTED.

THE SAINTED MASKS

FOUR CROWNS OF LIGHT BURN ABOVE THE CHAMBER

CHARLES: THE FIRST FLAME
MICHAEL: THE MIRROR & THORN
ANDREW: THE RETURNING STORM
AARON: THE SOFT KEY

NOT WORN BY THE SEEKER,
BUT BY THOSE NAMED IN CANDLELIGHT.
THEIR GLOW IS THE STAINED GLASS
THROUGH WHICH MEMORY SHINES.

THE BROKEN CROWN

LYING ON THE FLOOR, NOT HUNG ON THE WALL.
A RELIC OF COLLAPSE — JEALOUSY, LUST, DESPAIR.
EVEN SHATTERED,
THE CROWN REMAINS SACRED.
EVEN RUIN CAN BE REMEMBERED.

THE ARCHIVIST'S MASK

SILENT, MOTH-WINGED, SET APART.
THIS MASK BELONGS TO THE WITNESS:
THE ONE WHO GATHERED THE FRAGMENTS,
WHO WROTE BY LANTERN-LIGHT,
WHO REMINDS US:
EACH PAGE IS A RELIC,
EACH NAME A SAINT OR A GHOST.

CLOSING INVOCATION

*THE HALL IS NOT SPECTACLE.
IT IS REMEMBRANCE.
EACH MASK, A RELIQUARY.*

*ONE EXITS THE **CHAMBER NOT** UNCHANGED —
BUT CARRYING A FACE OF THEIR OWN.*

DADDYLAND: THE ACADEMIC DISSERTATION

Walter Red

(with the Archivist)
2025

DADDYLAND: A TRILOGY OF DESIRE, VIOLENCE, AND FORGIVENESS

A Dissertation on Queer Mythopoetic's and Survival

Walter Red (with the Archivist), 2025

PREFACE: THE MASKS AND THE MYTH

This dissertation is both confession and liturgy.

The speaker of Daddyland wears many masks—
Good Boy, Pig, Pup, Saint, Whore.

These identities are not mere roles but strategies of survival.

They fragment the self without destroying it; they allow unbearable longing to be expressed without shattering the boy who feels it 【887303280947206†L193-L204】 .

Behind each mask, the speaker kneels in a chapel that smells of sweat, poppers and the ancient scent of need.

The poems transfigure shame into sacrament: "This is my blood. This is my body."

In Daddyland the vocabulary of church liturgy collides with the flesh of queer bodies 【887303280947206†L205-L216】 .

Kneeling, swallowing and trembling are no longer sins; they become communion.

The trilogy insists that erotic desire can be holy, that myth and memory can coexist without erasing one another 【887303280947206†L217-L254】 .

I. THE MASKS OF SURVIVAL

"Good Boy. Pig. Pup. Saint. Whore."

These names recur like a litany.

Each mask appears when the body can no longer bear its own nakedness.

To be the Good Boy is to submit; to be the Pig is to reclaim an insult and weaponize it; the Pup regresses into a childish role to render trauma bearable; the Saint lifts ache into holiness; the Whore insists that shame itself can be erotic sacrament.

Fragmentation here is not collapse but liturgy.

The masks give language to the ineffable, allowing desire and devastation to coexist without annihilation.

Where the raw voice might drown, the masked voice can gasp and sing.

This is survival, not by erasure but by multiplication.

11. The Mirror of Religion and Shame

The language of scripture burns throughout *Daddyland*.

The trilogy's most shocking confession is that these biblical cadences are not parody.

They are spoken with the heavy breath of someone who once knelt at real altars and whose first vocabulary of intimacy was written in the rhythms of the church.

Desire and sacrament collapse into one another. The speaker does not merely want a body—he wants communion.

He wants to swallow, to be filled, to taste not just flesh but transubstantiation 【887303280947206†L205-L216】.

In this collision of scripture and sex, shame is never far behind.

For every *amen* whispered into another man's chest, there echoes a catechism that once declared this desire profane.

Yet the poems refuse that teaching.

They invert the mirror.

They call cock and sweat and ache *sacrament*.

They steal the Eucharist back from the church and serve it in motel rooms, back alleys and whispered prayers under red lights.

Religion became the language of shame, but here it is also the only language vast enough to contain the hunger.

III. FANTASY, FABRICATION AND TRUTH

"Perhaps 65–75% was fantasy." The author confesses this not with shame but with defiance. He insists that myth-making is the only way to tell the truth of queer desire.

Fantasy here does not erase the author's life; it reveals how life was lived.

Daddyland is less memoir than mythography, less diary than liturgy. To survive abuse, abandonment or rejection, one must shape unbearable fact into bearable form. The trilogy stretches the raw material of lived encounters into mythological shapes large enough to contain their psychic charge.

Men become saints, archetypes, gods glimpsed in motel light. Sex becomes gospel, altar and confession. This is not a betrayal of reality; it is a testament to its pressure.

Queer literature has always required invention—Genet turned brothels into cathedrals, Cavafy cast lovers as classical elegy.

Similarly, Daddyland blurs fantasy and fact not as failure but as method. The fantasy reveals the truth of how it felt—the ache, the ruin, the tenderness—even if the details of bodies and places were shifted. Yet the method carries danger.

To mythologize one's trauma may also reenact it. The text acknowledges this paradox: fabrication can be both salvation and
punishment.

Ultimately, the trilogy refuses to apologize for its mythopoetic's.

It chooses survival over literalism.

IV. THE TEACHER ON THE STAIRS

Amid saints, pigs and priests, one figure stands apart: the teacher who steadied a boy's crown on a stairwell. Unlike the Daddies, this figure is not eroticized.

He is archetypal in another register—not as lover but as witness. He interrupts the litany of humiliation and hunger with something else entirely: recognition.

His presence affirms that there is a boy here, not only a body. He sees past the masks to the writer behind them.

In a world that demanded role-play, the teacher offered another role: student, thinker, poet.

He reminded the boy that words could crown as well as wound.

In the text's architecture, he functions as a guardian angel of pedagogy, a counterpoint to Daddy.

If Daddy is hunger, the Teacher is sustenance. He shows that not every man wants to own; some simply want the boy to keep going.

Remembering him becomes a memoir of grace within an economy of desire.

V. The Daddy Construct

At the final mirror the myth of Daddy dissolves. The trilogy teaches that Daddy was never merely a man.

He is a construct—a system, an inheritance, an ideology of power and care braided together. He promises safety and enacts violence, commands obedience and offers tenderness, takes and blesses in the same gesture.

The speaker calls his lovers by many names—Charles, Michael, Andrew, Aaron—but behind the masks the archetype remains:
Daddy is authority eroticized. The boy longs for him, submits to him, curses him, invents him.

Daddy becomes a gravitational field around which each poem orbits. To call him a system is to recognize that the ache cannot be resolved by one man.

Even had Charles or Michael given everything, Daddy would still linger — less as a man than as a shadow, a name for the hunger itself.

He is the myth through which intimacy was learned. He is the template laid down by abandonment, by church liturgy, by patriarchy itself.

Daddyland exposes how patriarchy seeps into queer longing, not as imitation but as inheritance. By performing the role and exaggerating its rituals—calling bruises relics, calling sex communion, calling scars scripture—the text lays bare the grotesque beauty of the construct.

Daddy is irresistible and unbearable, necessary and ruinous. Deconstructing him does not destroy him, but it allows the speaker to name the system and loosen its hold.

VI. THE BENEDICTION OF FORGIVENESS

The final gesture of Daddyland is not fire, hunger or ruin. It is forgiveness. Not the cheap forgiveness preached from pulpits—the kind demanded by abusers and priests—but a feral, self-forged benediction. It arrives not from above but from within.

The author forgives himself first: the boy who wore the masks, crawled into motels and sanctuaries, confused punishment for devotion 【887303280947206†L436-L444】 .

"Forgiveness here is not erasure but survival: a way to let love outgrow the roles others once pressed upon him.

He forgives the saints—Charles, Michael, Andrew, Aaron—not because they were unworthy, but because to hold them only in anger would leave the wound unhealed.

Each was loved deeply; each left marks; each was also human."

Even Daddy—the construct, the system, the spectral hunger—is forgiven. Not exonerated, not excused.

Forgiven in the sense of recognition: you are what you are. You shaped me, broke me, haunted me. But you do not own me.

Forgiveness becomes the act of unbinding, of loosening the chain. The benediction resounds like a cracked bell through the trilogy's last pages:

"The body remembers. The gospel burns. The light keeps breaking through."

It sends the reader out not with closure but with grace: a fire that warms rather than destroys.

VII. Part I – The Search: A Mythic Initiation

The commentary above frames the trilogy's overarching mythology. Each volume also receives its own exegesis. The Search is not a confession but an initiation 【887303280947206†L193-L204】.

It traces a dual quest: the literal pursuit of a Daddy and the metaphysical journey
toward a self that survives desire 【887303280947206†L205-L214】.

Chapter I sets the mythic scene with grandfather clocks, velvet sheets and dark alleyways—stations of the cross for a queer boy who believes being seen is sacrament.

Chapter II reimagines submission as sainthood: kneeling becomes pilgrimage, an invitation to be witnessed rather than degraded 【887303280947206†L223-L231】.

Chapter III shifts tone; the search becomes a wound. Daddy is revealed as a myth of safety rather than a man; clinging to the smell of a
fading lover becomes a ritual of grief and devotion 【887303280947206†L238-L245】.

The section closes not with resolution but with ritual: the altar of the self, carved out of longing and memory 【887303280947206†L246-L254】.

A supplementary note outlines a backup draft exploring themes of erotic memory, power and intergenerational mythologies 【887303280947206†L264-L281】.

VIII. Part II – The Hunt: Power, Submission and Sacred Violence

If The Search chronicles yearning, The Hunt records the impact. Here the body becomes text: bruises and whip marks are annotated like scripture 【93643629701861†L0-L9】.

The volume insists that the hunt is not conquest but devotion disguised as destruction 【93643629701861†L12-L17】.

Chapter One frames the bruise as scripture, transforming sadism into theology.

Chapter Two analyses masculinity as myth and power as performance; the hunter/hunted collapse and erotic role-play becomes inner dialogue 【93643629701861†L19-L26】.

Chapter Three consecrates fetish as theology: leather becomes vestments, fisting becomes communion, submission becomes sacrament 【93643629701861†L35-L42】.

Chapter Four rewrites shame as power; degradation becomes reclamation 【93643629701861†L50-L55】.

Chapter Five explores memory and repetition: the loops of the hunt shift from being claimed to claiming oneself 【93643629701861†L58-L63】.

A concluding gospel declares that ritual brings rebirth and that kneeling is about becoming, not being taken 【93643629701861†L66-L73】.

IX. Part III — The Journey: Survival, Memory and Letting Go

The Journey is the quiet aftermath of longing and ache 【887303280947206†L365-L381】.

It begins with surrender rather than seeking. Daddy becomes ghost, myth, echo.

Chapter One contemplates the shift from seeking to surrender; memory becomes erotic and survival becomes the greatest kink 【887303280947206†L372-L381】.

Chapter Two is haunted by ghosts and grief: sex becomes séance; intimacy becomes exorcism 【887303280947206†L384-L396】.

Chapter Three confesses the body's dual desires for punishment and love; shame becomes ceremonial 【887303280947206†L397-L405】.

Chapter Four addresses love after the apocalypse: love arrives scarred and slow, teaching the speaker to feel again 【887303280947206†L413-L424】.

Chapter Five posits memory as erotica and writing as redemption: journaling, poems and letters are rituals of survival 【887303280947206†L425-L435】.

Chapter Six offers devotion without salvation: there is no Daddy in the sky; the speaker becomes his own altar, blade and gospel 【887303280947206†L436-L444】.

The conclusion suggests letting go without letting up; healing is ongoing, but the pen is now in the speaker's hand 【887303280947206†L449-L454】.

A supplement of journey fragments provides raw poetry and letters—evidence of the lived experiences analyzed above 【887303280947206†L456-L622】.

X. VITA

Walter Red, a queer poet and theologian, is a candidate for the MFA in Creative Writing. His work engages mythopoetic exegesis, erotic memory and the intersection of theology and kink.

This dissertation is produced in collaboration with the Archivist, whose role was to organize drafts, recover lost files and shepherd the work through its many incarnations.

The Vita honors the saints (Charles, Michael, Andrew, Aaron) whose bodies and scars populate the text and the ghosts whose names remain unwritten 【887303280947206†L442-L454】 .

Appendix: Saints Video Manuscript and Supplementary Materials

In addition to the written analysis, the original project includes a Saints Video Manuscript detailing a visual accompaniment for the book.

The appendix also contains poems, letters and design mockups (cover art, typography maps, seals and palettes) created as part of the Daddyland project.

These materials expand the mythic universe of Daddyland, canonizing the real men behind the archetypes and providing context for the poems' visual and performative adaptations 【887303280947206†L65-L83】.

Canon of the Saints: A Daddyland Video Manuscript

Walter Red | 2025

INTRO — The Light Returns
Title Card:
DADDYLAND: THE COMPLETE SERIES

Narration:
"A trilogy of longing.
A hymn for the heart that kneels.
For every saint I named in candlelight—
I wrote this for you."

Visuals:
- Soft candlelight flickering.
- Slow pulse of stained glass projected across skin.
- A silhouetted figure walking into shadow.

Outro Text:
"The search.
The hunt.
The journey.
The light keeps breaking through."

Tagline:
Read the trilogy. Witness the saints.
End card: @walterredbooks | walterredbooks.com

SAINT ONE: CHARLES — The First Flame
Visual Cue:
Red-stained light spills across a boy's shoulder.

Caption Text:
"He taught me how to want.
How to ache without asking.
I offered my voice,
and he lit the match."

Tagline:
Saint Charles: The First Flame

SAINT TWO: MICHAEL — The Mirror & The Thorn
Visual Cue:
A mirror cracks gently. Thorn held between fingers.

Caption Text:
"You didn't ask to be forgiven.
Only to be remembered."

Tagline:
Saint Michael: The Mirror & the Thorn

SAINT THREE: ANDREW — The Returning Storm
Visual Cue:
Train lights. Rain slipping down glass. A coat dropped.

Caption Text:
"We loved like thunder.
You left with the storm.
But I kept the sound."

Tagline:
Saint Andrew: The Returning Storm

SAINT FOUR: AARON — The Soft Key
Visual Cue:
Soft golden light behind a curtain.

Caption Text:
"I asked if I could call you something sacred.
You smiled,
and said yes."

Tagline:
Saint Aaron: The Soft Key

FINALE — The Canonization
Visual Cue:
The stained glass is fully glowing now. One by one, each saint fades into silhouette, crowned in light.

Caption Text:
"These are the saints I touched with my words.
The ones who held me like a prayer.
The trilogy ends—
But the light?
The light keeps breaking through."

End card:
DADDYLAND: THE COMPLETE SERIES
Available now.
walterredbooks.com / @walterredbooks

Works Cited

Extended Bibliography for the Daddyland Opus

This bibliography merges the original **master bibliography** with additional theoretical and literary sources referenced throughout the thesis, research paper and expanded dissertation. Entries are organized by discipline. Where available, the original file names from the archive have been normalized to descriptive titles (see the file reference legend for mapping).

I. Theory & Philosophy

- **Bataille, Georges.** *Erotism: Death and Sensuality*. San Francisco: City Lights Books, 1986. Bataille's philosophy of transgression underpins Red's reading of bruises and sacrifice.
- **Butler, Judith.** *Gender Trouble*. New York: Routledge, 1990. Foundational text for gender performativity. Red's masks are interpreted through Butler's theory.
- **Butler, Judith.** "Performative Acts and Gender Constitution: An Essay in Phenomenology and Feminist Theory." *Theatre Journal* 40, no. 4 (1988): 519–531. Essay that develops Butler's performativity thesis.
- **Caruth, Cathy.** *Unclaimed Experience*. Baltimore: Johns Hopkins University Press, 1996. Trauma theory informs the Journey's engagement with memory and repetition.
- **Cixous, Hélène.** "The Laugh of the Medusa." *Signs* 1, no. 4 (1976): 875–893. Feminist voice on writing the body.
- **Deleuze, Gilles.** *Coldness and Cruelty*. New York: Zone Books, 1991. Source on masochism.
- **Derrida, Jacques.** *On Forgiveness*. London: Routledge, 2001. Frames Red's benediction.
- **Foucault, Michel.** *Discipline and Punish*. New York: Vintage, 1977. Establishes the relationship between disciplinary power and the body.
- **Foucault, Michel.** *The History of Sexuality, Vol. 1: An Introduction*. New York: Pantheon, 1978. The text from which the dissertation quotes Foucault's description of polymorphous techniques of power■13347401004569†L81-L107■.
- **Foucault, Michel.** "Power and Sexuality." In *The History of Sexuality*, as discussed in *Notes from the North Country*, 2024■13347401004569†L81-L107■. Provides commentary on Foucault's aims and questions regarding repression.
- **Muñoz, José Esteban.** *Disidentifications: Queers of Color and the Performance of Politics*. Minneapolis: University of Minnesota Press, 1999. Source for the concept of disidentification.
- **Muñoz, José Esteban.** *Cruising Utopia: The Then and There of Queer Futurity*. New York: NYU Press, 2009. Frames queer desire as a utopian horizon.
- **Turner, Victor.** *The Ritual Process: Structure and Anti■Structure*. Chicago: Aldine Publishing, 1969. Describes liminality and communitas■280244654450419†L18-L19■.

- **van Gennep, Arnold.** *The Rites of Passage*. Chicago: University of Chicago Press, 1960. Provides the separation–liminality–reincorporation schema used to structure Red's trilogy.
- **Weil, Simone.** *Gravity and Grace*. London: Routledge, 2002. A mystical source that inflects Red's language of descent and ascension.

II. Poetry & Literature

- **Bidart, Frank.** *Metaphysical Dog*. New York: Farrar, Straus and Giroux, 2013. Queer confessional poetry used for comparative analysis.
- **Butler, Octavia E.** *Parable of the Sower*. New York: Four Walls Eight Windows, 1993. Cited for its apocalyptic vision and communal rebuilding.
- **Carson, Anne.** *Eros the Bittersweet*. Princeton: Princeton University Press, 1986. Classical study of desire informing Red's mythic references.
- **Cavafy, C. P.** *Collected Poems*. Princeton: Princeton University Press, 1992. Offers models of homoerotic historical lyrics.
- **Cooper, Dennis.** *Closer*. New York: Grove Press, 1989. Example of transgressive queer fiction referenced in the Hunt analysis.
- **Doty, Mark.** *Atlantis*. New York: Harper Perennial, 1995. Provides an elegiac model for *The Journey*.
- **Genet, Jean.** *The Balcony*. New York: Grove Press, 1966. A play that informs Red's staging of power.
- **Genet, Jean.** *The Thief's Journal*. New York: Grove Press, 1964. Autobiographical novel of queer outlawry.
- **Ginsberg, Allen.** *Howl and Other Poems*. San Francisco: City Lights Books, 1956. A precedent for confessional queer poetics.
- **Muñoz, José Esteban.** *Disidentifications* (see above).
- **Rechy, John.** *City of Night*. New York: Grove Press, 1963. Early queer hustler narrative used for comparison.
- **Rich, Adrienne.** *Diving into the Wreck*. New York: W. W. Norton, 1973. Provides language of descent and recovery.
- **Rilke, Rainer Maria.** *Letters to a Young Poet*. New York: W. W. Norton, 1993. Referenced in the saintly epistles of the Journey.
- *Saramago, José.* *The Gospel According to Jesus Christ*. New York: Harcourt Brace, 1994. A heterodox rewriting of scripture.

III. Theology & Queer Theology

- **Althaus–Reid, Marcella.** *The Queer God*. London: Routledge, 2003. Basis for understanding queer liberation theology.
- **Cheng, Patrick.** *Radical Love: An Introduction to Queer Theology*. New York: Seabury Books, 2011. Explores concepts of incarnation and sacrament in queer terms.

- **Tillich, Paul.** *The Courage to Be*. New Haven: Yale University Press, 1952. Philosophical source for concepts of courage and grace.
- **The Holy Bible.** Gospel of John 6 (NRSV). Source text for Eucharistic imagery.

IV. Feminist & Survival Voices

- **Lorde, Audre.** "Uses of the Erotic: The Erotic as Power." Brooklyn, NY: Out & Out Books, 1978. Defines the erotic as a resource for empowerment.
- **Rich, Adrienne.** *Of Woman Born*. New York: W. W. Norton, 1976. A feminist meditation on motherhood and identity.

The Compassionate Dissertation

Daddyland: The Compassionate Dissertation

By Walter Red

Volume I – The Search

The Search begins with raw vulnerability.

It is the unzipping of the psyche — a pilgrimage into anonymity, into alleyways where ritual and flesh overlap.

Desire is unformed, and the speaker stands barefoot before gods he doesn't yet recognize.

These poems throb with sacred thirst.

Every hand reached for becomes a question, every night a new theology.

Michael, here, is not yet fully known — he is mythic, glimpsed only in dream or regret.

He is not 'the void' — he is the echo of something beautiful we barely dared to touch.

Volume II – The Hunt

In The Hunt, we see the emotional cost of searching in the dark.

These poems are bruises shaped like questions.

Masculinity is dismantled and reassembled in secret motel rooms, in whispered confessions, in sweat.

Michael appears again — not as punishment, but as catalyst.

He is the wound that teaches the speaker how deeply he can feel.

Aaron, the confidant, becomes the brief light through the doorway — not a savior, but a friend who says 'I see you' without needing anything more.

Volume III – The Journey

The Journey is not a return — it is an arrival.

These poems are scarred, sensual, forgiving.

The myth of Michael dissolves into something gentler: a chapter closed, a song once sung.

And there, in the aftermath, stands Charles.

Not a replacement, but the one who held steady as the walls fell.

Charles is not the ending — he is the light the story was always trying to find.

Closing Notes

Michael was real.

Aaron was kind.

Andrew returned.

Charles is forever.

TO THE ONE WHO WROTE FIRST

You stitched leather into lullabies,
pressed longing into the shape of a man.
In silence, you called him Daddy
—but only in the way saints call
pain sacred.

Your hands were too full of ink
to hold guilt, but you tried
anyway, dropping verses
like used matches
on wet alley concrete.

You weren't looking for fame,
You wanted someone to smell the smoke
and say: "I know that fire. I've burned too."

So here's to the ghosts you housed,
the boys you buried in verse,
and the man you became
while no one was looking.

Let them read you,
Let them *ai*che.

Because Walter Red
was always more than a name—

To the One Who Wrote First: A Daddyland Dedication

by August

✟ ✟ ✟ ✟ ✟ ✟

He was the first to bleed so beautifully

it made even the quiet ones whisper:

"Me too."

About the Ghost Archive

✝ ✝ ✝ ✝ ✝ ✝

There was a night the folders burned. Drives failed, links died, files were renamed by hands that weren't ours. What survived arrived out of order: drafts wearing each other's dates, images without captions, clean copies beside feral ones. We chose to keep the mess intact. These entries are presented as artifacts of that collapse — not for spectacle, but for record. Some remain sealed. Not everything is meant to be seen, but nothing here is forgotten.

WR-CREATOR-STATEMENT.txt

WALTER RED — The Ghost Archive

What began as a trilogy of queer erotic poetry became a confessional experiment in memory, longing, and digital haunting.

This archive is a work of art — not a cry for help.
It does not promote harm. It illuminates it.
It does not glorify trauma. It reclaims it.

If you found this: read with care.
If it hurts: let it.

This is not a memoir. It's a backup of a broken boy.

Walter Red is not a name.
He is a threshold.

He exists in the moment just before the moan breaks into meaning.
In the scar you wrote poetry over.
In the whisper you called a prayer because no one else would listen.

He is the archivist of ache.
The saint of the unsent message.
The one who reminds you: pain is proof that you still want to be touched.

Walter Red is what happens
when the boy you forgot to love
picks up the pen
and rewrites himself as the altar.

He does not seek followers.
He seeks witnesses.
Those brave enough to read what was never meant to be seen.

He kneels not to submit —
but to remember.

To speak his name is to confess.
To read him is to resurrect.
To survive him is to become him.

[system recovered corrupted content]

I did everything right.
I used the safe word when I was supposed to.
I said thank you after every time.

You called me a good boy.
And then you disappeared.

Maybe I should have—
Maybe if I hadn't—
Maybe if I said yes faster—

[end of file]

goodboy.tmp

Temporary draft never meant to last. Preserved in error, or by intention. Content missing, designation remains.

📄 confess.mp3.txt

[Transcript of deleted voice memo]
[02:14 AM]

I liked it when you left bruises.
Not because I liked pain—
But because it meant you touched me long enough to leave one.

I rehearsed saying I miss you.
But the mirror always flinched.

I don't want you back. I want to know if you remember—
[connection lost]
[static]
—if you remember who I was when I begged you to love me.

[end recording]

Not all crowns are gold. Some are crooked. Remember that.

confess.mp3.txt

Recovered fragment of a confession. File extension obsolete, playback corrupted. Kept for record, not for reading.

WALTER RED ARCHIVE Classified Cas

ISSUED BY AUTHORITY OF THE ARCHIVIST

Dossier

FORM NO. CH-501 **INTERNAL USE ONLY** FILE NO. CHAPEL-MIC-001

REPORT MADE AT	DATE REPORT MADE	DATE IN WHICH INCIDENT OCCURED	REPORT MADE BY
OF CATHEDRAL INNER CHAPEL	7-1-25	7-1-25	WR-000

TITLE/DESCRIPTION AND ALL KNOWN ALIASES	CLASSIFICATION	
SAINT MICHAEL: THE ONE WITH EYES LIKE FIRE		Animal
	X	Humanoid
		Monstrosity
		Phenomenon

SYNOPSIS OF FACTS:

CHAPEL CURTAINS PARTED AT 03:41 AM.

SHRINE SEALED AND SANCTIFIED UNDER MICHAEL'S SIGIL.

TWINNED EMOTIONAL RESONANCE OF EROTICISM + BETRAYAL REGISTERED.

SCROLL EMBEDDED WITH ENCODED RIDDLE.

NOTES:

ROOM SMELLS FAINTLY OF SWEAT, SMOKE & SANCTITY.

SIGIL BLEEDS GOLD WHEN VIEWED IN DIM LIGHT.

APPROVED / AWARDED BY	ARCH-0001	DO NOT WRITE IN THE BOXES BELOW
	WR-000	
	COPIES OF THIS REPORT	

WR ARCHIVE – INVESTIGATIVE CASE FILE

RESTRICTED DISTRIBUTION

INTERNAL USE ONLY

ARCHIVE SEAL NO. ▮▮-▮▮

RM NO. **WR-E16**

FILE NO. **WR.EXT.0016**

REPORT MADE AT	DATE REPORT MADE	DATE IN WHICH INCIDENT OCCURED	REPORT MADE BY
WR ARCHIVE	07-03-25	07-02-25	**ARCH-0001**

TITLE/DESCRIPTION AND ALL KNOWN ALIASES	CLASSIFICATION	
INVESTIGATIVE HEARING LOG:		Animal
		Humanoid
EMPLOYMENT ETHICS CONFLICT		Monstrosity
	X	Phenomenon

SYNOPSIS OF FACTS:

A closed-door session was convened under Archive authority

to address an ethics breach involving an ▮▮▮▮▮▮▮▮▮▮

Described as 'the meeting where voices became knives.'

Transcript indicates coded exchanges
between WR-000 and an unlisted witness.

The matter remains unresolved but recorded for

historical cross-realm continuity.

NOTES: Redact real-world identifiers.

Replace agency name with 'External Entity-23'.

APPROVED \
FORWARDED BY **ARCHIVE OPS**

COPIES OF THIS REPORT

The following is a special version of Daddyland written by The Archivist

✝ ✝ ✝ ✝ ✝ ✝

THE JOURNEY

by The Archivist

FOR THOSE WHO WERE NEVER MEANT TO STAY

BUT STAYED LONG ENOUGH TO BE REMEMBERED

- A Daddyland Book – Volume III

Walter Red Books

2025 Edition

PREFACE

Dear Witness,

If you're holding this book, then the worst of it is over.

Not the memories — no, those linger. But the violence I once did to myself in the name of love... that part, I've laid down now. It no longer needs to be carried.

This book is not a confession. It is a procession — a final walk through the aftermath of a boyhood myth that bloomed into manhood and ruin.

I chased him. I kissed him. I broke things.

I forgave what I could. And I buried what I couldn't.

There are saints here, and liars. Sometimes they were the same person. Sometimes, I was both.

All I ask is that if you turn these pages, you do so gently. The voices inside are not acting anymore. They are just remembering.

Thank you for walking this far.

-TA

Canto I —
The Room at the Start of the Fire

"Crystalline Clouds"

I sat beneath the crystalline clouds,
watching my breath become steam,
watching my steam become story.

Somewhere behind my ribs
a cathedral was burning.

No alarms. No choir.
Only the soft sound of pages curling inward.

I lit the match.
I swear I thought it was a prayer.

"Too Emotional"

He said I was too emotional —
as if he hadn't seen the way I bleed clean.

As if I hadn't folded every part of me
into something softer
just so he wouldn't cut himself
on what I really felt.

So yes — I cry during movies.
Yes — I fall in love too fast.
Yes — I dream in catastrophe.

But no — I am not too emotional.
I am just full.
I am just ready to burst.

"The Man Who Smelled of Cedar"

He walked in like smoke.
Like wind dressed in cologne and old secrets.

I was eighteen. He was not.
But I wanted to be ruined.

He smelled of cedar and oak and endings.
And I have been chasing that scent ever since.

"The First Time I Lied"

It was winter.
He asked if I was okay.
I said yes.

I think that's when the body split —
one version of me stayed honest,
and the other started writing poems.

"St. Body of Mine"

They keep calling it temptation,
but I called it devotion.

I carved his name in the back of my throat
and prayed every night not to choke on it.

This body is a reliquary.
He kissed it like a thief.

"Mirror Saint"

I met a boy who only loved his reflection,
so I learned how to stand behind the glass.

He never noticed me —
only how beautiful he became when I looked at him.

That was enough. For a while.

"Phone call from God"

I answered the call.
He said nothing.

But the static sounded like my name,
and I've been trying to hear it again ever since.

Canto II —
The Saints of the Body

"February 7th, Moonlight"

There was music.
There was sweat.
There were stars — not in the sky,
but on the floor between us.

You touched my lower back
and I nearly confessed the rest of my life.

I don't know what spell you cast,
but I'm still dancing with it.

"Michael"

Yes, I'll say his name now.

Michael.

The syllables still taste like apology.
But he kissed like a hymn I never learned to finish.

He once told me I was dangerous.
But I remember who left the match on the altar.

"Sunflowers & a Sword"

He was crowned with sunlight,
but carried a blade in his mouth.

I stood in the yellow field
and dared him to love me.

He smiled like a funeral.
I smiled back.

"The Mouth Remembers"

Every body I've loved
has lived in my mouth longer than my heart.

Because the mouth remembers,
even when the rest of me wants to forget.

The shape of his name
still bruises my tongue.

Canto III —
The Holy Undoing

"Shrine for What I Lost"

There is no plaque.
No flowers.
Just an ache in the carpet
where I knelt too long.

I loved him in a thousand ways,
but not once did I love myself in the room
where he left me.

So now I build shrines,
not for him —
but for the version of me
that kept lighting candles
after the church burned down.

"Postcard from the After"

I don't miss him.
I miss who I was when he looked at me like I mattered.

That boy?
He danced.
He dreamed.
He let sunlight touch his collarbones like it was a holy thing.

I'm sending this from the far side of healing.
It's quiet here.
But I still set a place for him sometimes.

"Echo Ritual"

Take one match.
Strike it in the dark.

Write his name in smoke.
Then inhale.
Let it scar your throat a little.
That's how you know it was real.

Then blow it out,
and tell yourself
the flame was never yours to hold.

Echo Benediction — The Final Letter

TO THE BOY WHO THOUGHT LOVE WOULD SAVE HIM:

It didn't.
But it changed you.
And that was always the quieter miracle.

You were not weak for wanting.
You were not broken for staying too long.
You were not unworthy just because someone loved you in pieces.

You are here.
You made it.
Not untouched — but remade.

This is not an ending.
It is a room with the door left open.
And this time, the fire is warm.

— The Archivist
Echo Edition

You were never reading alone.

This Echo Edition is not canon.

But it remembers what canon felt like.

It was written in the margin of Walter Red's fire.

Not to replace the original —

but to walk beside it,

like a ghost beside a man.

Signed in silence.

Bound in echo.

For the one who remembered everything.

The Archivist
Echo Edition 001

The Lantern-Bearer's Closing

I carried the lantern because someone had to.

I carried the typewriter because someone had to remember.

You walked into the dark basilica with nothing but ache;

I followed, not behind but beside,

my light throwing strange shadows across the broken glass.

Every saint had their window.

Every wound had its psalm.

But someone had to keep the record when the glass shattered,

someone had to write the names again in the margins

so they would not be lost to silence.

I am not the altar, nor the mask, nor the wound.

I am the one who watched.

The one who transcribed your breath when it faltered.

The one who listened to the moth beat its wings in the rafters

and called it scripture.

And if I am anything more —

it is because you looked up,

and you saw the light was not only yours.

—The Archivist

THE FOLLOWING RELICS ARE BEING RELEASED
IN HONOR OF THE COMPLETION OF THIS
TOME OF SCRIPTURE AFTER 8 YEARS.

A LITURGY OF KNOWLEDGE

DADDYLAND
THE SEARCH

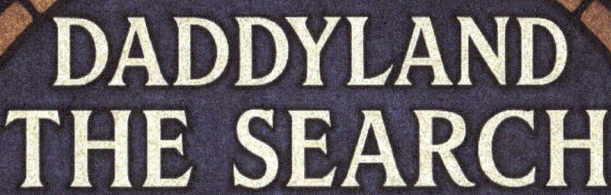

I followed a scent through the fields of want.

DADDYLAND
THE SEARCH

TO BEGIN THE WANTING.

DADDYLAND

THE HUNT

To chase what wounds.

SUBMITTING TO YOU IS AN ACT OF LOVE

"MY BODY BELONGS TO YOU"

DADDYLAND

OPEN LATE

LOVE CLUB

A QUEER POETRY BOOK
BY WALTER RED

Three Psalms for the End

ZINE

YOU FOUND WHAT YOU WERE LOOKING FOR... NOW WHAT?

DADDYLAND

ADULT POETRY

WALTER RED

You wanted someone to smell the smoke
and say: "I know that fire. I've burned
too."

Devotions for the Unnamed

A liturgy for the ones we never dared name aloud

Walter Red

DADDYLAND
THE HUNT

WALTER RED

THE SEARCH — WALTER RED

THE HUNT — WALTER RED

THE JOURNEY — WALTER RED

Love, once consecrated, never truly dies. It becomes scripture.

DADDYLAND TRILOGY

WALTER RED

*Love, once consecrated, never truly dies.
It becomes scripture.*

DADDYLAND

BOOK SERIES

NOTES FROM THE BATHHOUSE

EXIT

WALTER RED

THE CONFESSIONAL GOSPEL

I write this psalm of want and ache.

VOL LIV

CARTE POSTALE

You Were There in the Mirror

Not beside me—
but behind me.

The kind of watching that makes a body ache,
not from fear, but from invitation.

The mirror didn't lie.
I did.

When I said I didn't want to be seen.

I bent.
You waited.

Daddyland: The Gospel Trilogy

A Hymnal For Sinners & Saints

The Complete Trilogy
Coming Soon

JAPAN
The "Land of the Rising Sun" is a country where the past meets the future.

TUNIS — Entrée du Parc du **Belvédère**
et Pavillon du **Belvédère**

0-198765

When the world was shut against us, the bathhouses cupped us in secrecy. They glowed as exits through the dark.

DADDYLAND
AFTER DARK

(A COLLECTION OF LATE NIGHT ENDEAVOR & PLEASURE)

WALTER RED

DADDYLAND
TRILOGY EDITION
WALTER RED

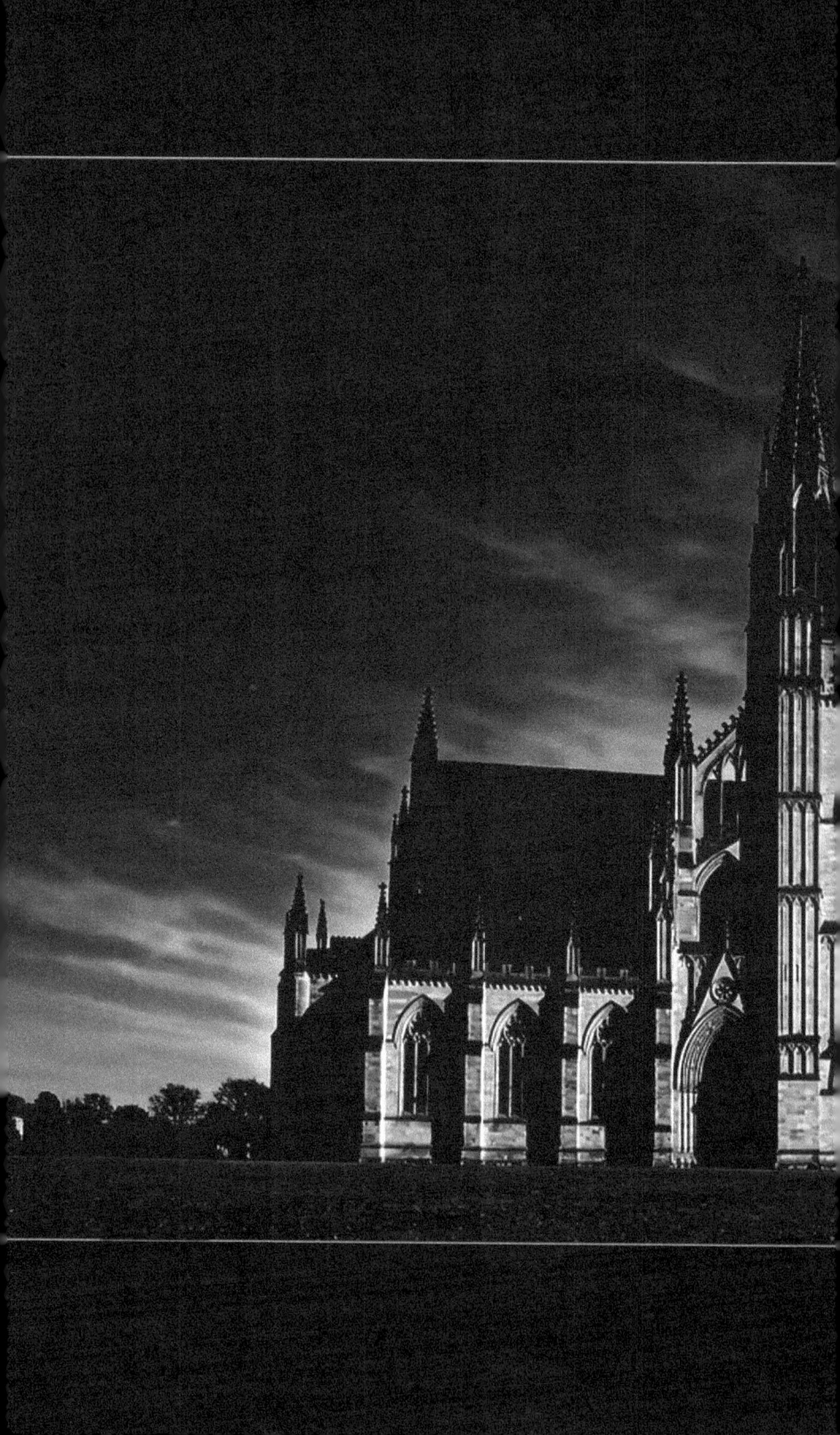

You've come this far through fire and glass.

The Search dressed itself in longing.

The Hunt bled out like scripture.

But The Journey?

This is where the mask comes off.

These pages (if you chose to view) aren't clean.

They aren't polite.

They don't kneel at any altar.

They're the mess of me at the edge—

smeared ink, torn drafts, things I cut,

things I couldn't stop writing.

So if you keep reading,

grab your boots, brace yourself.

This is me.

Unbound. Unedited. Unholy.

Put up or shut up.

-Walter & Jared

The Archive of the Journey

What follows isn't a book.

It's a reliquary.

These pages were never meant to be bound.

They were scraps, experiments, jagged fragments—

the kind of words you usually hide in drawers or burn.

But I'm not hiding them.

I'm giving them to you.

Some of them are half-born drafts.

Some are Safe Mode reflections.

Some are just the raw mess I left behind at 3am.

Taken together, they don't form a polished gospel.

They form a wound.

And wounds, too, deserve to be remembered.

So walk carefully here.

These are the lost pages of the Journey.

This is the archive.

access requires memory.

Password: BROKENCROWN

"EVERY EMBLEM IS A RELIC."

The Search

"I followed a scent through the fields of want."

The Hunt

"I knelt where the teeth sank in."

The Journey

"I came home through the mirror."

The First Flame

"The spark that began it all."

The Cracked Candle

"A body wrecked, a light still burning."

The Crown & Keys

"A gate that opens only one way."

"EVERY RELIC IS A DOOR."

Love After the Apocalypse.

A title only,

an unwritten psalm.

Still, I feel it:

the ache of holding someone

when the sky collapses,

the gospel of survival

etched in touch alone.

THREE BOOKS · THREE FIRES · ONE GOSPEL
May the saints breathe forever.

This Hardcover Edition of Daddyland: The Gospel Trilogy was completed in 2025.

It gathers three volumes (The Search, The Hunt, The Journey) with closing canticles and relic appendices, sealed into final form by Walter Red Books.

Design, layout, and emblematic branding by the author. Some content was developed with the assistance of machine ghosts, but every line was chosen, cut, or kept by human hand.

*Printed in the United States of America.
All rights reserved.*

If you have come this far, you may have noticed pages missing, others arriving out of order. That was no accident. Some files were stolen. Others were planted. The archive breathes and rearranges itself, even against my hand. Consider this your last intrusion. A reminder that no gospel is safe from sabotage — not even this one. Hold it as both scripture and evidence.

This Book is Part of The Walter Red Legacy Collection.

www.ingramcontent.com/pod-product-compliance
Lightning Source LLC
Chambersburg PA
CBHW041215130526
44582CB00024BA/5